Robert White is a student of history and a man with a heart for Christian revival. He has done a masterful job of outlining the deepest spiritual needs of this hour, but he does more than list the problems of our godless culture. He offers a complete biblical solution—and then he passionately calls us to respond in prayer. This is a book you should read while on your knees.

—J. Lee Grady, Editor
Charisma Magazine

AWAKE AMERICA!

ROBERT WHITE

CREATION HOUSE
A STRANG COMPANY

Awake, America! by Robert White
Published by Creation House
A Strang Company
600 Rinehart Road
Lake Mary, Florida 32746
www.creationhouse.com

Design Director: Bill Johnson
Cover Designer: Marvin Eans

Library of Congress Control Number: 2008923864
International Standard Book Number: 978-1-59979-370-2

09 10 11 12 — 98765432
Printed in the United States of America

We have grown in numbers, wealth and power, as no other nation has ever grown. But we have forgotten God. We have forgotten the gracious hand which preserved us in peace, and multiplied and enriched and strengthened us; and we have vainly imagined, in the deceitfulness of our hearts, that all these blessings were produced by some superior wisdom and virtue of our own. Intoxicated with unbroken success, we have become too self-sufficient to feel the necessity of redeeming and preserving grace, too proud to pray to the God that made us!

It behooves us then, to humble ourselves before the offended Power, to confess our national sins, and to pray for clemency and forgiveness.[1]

—Abraham Lincoln
March 30, 1863
Presidential Proclamation: National Fast Day

O beautiful for spacious skies,
For amber waves of grain,
For purple mountain majesties
Above the fruited plain!
America! America!
God shed His grace on thee,
And crown thy good with brotherhood
From sea to shining sea!

—"America the Beautiful"
by Katherine Lee Bates

DEDICATION

THIS BOOK IS DEDICATED TO MANY PEOPLE.

First, it is dedicated to God Himself, who anointed, blessed, provided, protected, and favored America in her embryonic stage when she was still in the womb of history; when the early settlers braved the dangers on the sea and then on land as they established settlements in a new and uncharted land. He watched over the early pioneers when thoughts of a new nation had not yet been born.

Second, this book is dedicated to those pioneers who settled this country at great hardship and sacrifice, but were driven by a vision of a land where free men and women would live and enjoy freedom of speech and religion.

Third, this book is dedicated to those great men who signed the Declaration of Independence, because all of them suffered great loss; some the loss of all their possessions, some the loss of families, and some the loss of life. They embodied the spirit demonstrated by Patrick Henry, who said, "Is life so dear, or peace so sweet, as to be purchased at the price of chains and slavery? Forbid it, almighty God!"[1]

Fourth, this book is dedicated to the undernourished, ill-equipped, ragtag army of the Revolution, who were outnumbered and under trained, yet refused to quit and refused to die until the battle was won; and to the framers of the Constitution, who were careful to see that freedom of speech and freedom of religion were incorporated into that great document.

Fifth, this book is dedicated to the men and women who fought in various wars on foreign soil to protect the freedoms won in the Revolutionary War, and to the families that gave up those great soldiers who paid the ultimate sacrifice to keep America free.

Sixth, this book is dedicated to the bold men and women of today who continue to speak out and stand up for God and for a free America. Their voices are unpopular with the proponents of political correctness, but their names will be inscribed on the hall of fame scroll of heaven because they, like Shadrach, Meshach, and Abednego, never bowed to the graven images of secularism, humanism, or the other gods of this world.

Seventh, this book is dedicated to the Holy Spirit, who is at work today in America lifting up the name of Jesus Christ. He is preparing the body of Christ to be ready for the soon return of the Bridegroom for His bride, the church of the living God. God's Holy Spirit is working to bring revival and a renewal of passion in the body of Christ to this great land!

AWAKE, AMERICA—THE VISION

I HAVE BEEN IN THE MINISTRY FOR OVER FIFTY YEARS and have experienced visions on only three occasions, the third of which took place September 1, 2001. I was in my bedroom about to retire for the night. I was not praying or reading the Bible. While sitting on the side of the bed, I suddenly saw a giant football field different from any other football field I had ever seen. Instead of two teams playing football, I saw several teams matched up by twos scattered over the field: two teams lined up against one another at one end of the field, another two teams matched up elsewhere. This configuration continued all over the field. Each set of teams was oblivious to the other teams on the field.

Then I looked to the stands. Rather than watching the teams on the field, the people were busy committing every type of crime imaginable: muggings, hold-ups, murders with knives and guns, and more. The stands were filled with drug dealers, prostitutes, thieves, and murderers, none of whom ever looked at any time toward the field.

The isolation between the stands and the teams on the field struck me forcefully. The teams were oblivious to what was happening in the stands, completely unaware of the sin and hurting people.

Finally, as I continued to survey the panoramic view of the stands, I saw the devil sitting there. He never spoke, but his eyes were glued to the playing field. There was just the hint of a smile on his face as he seemed to be satisfied with what he saw.

It was then that the Lord spoke to me, revealing to me what I saw. The teams on the playing field were the churches; the people in the stands were a hurting world. The Lord told me that the teams were more focused on competing with one another than they were in reaching out to and helping the hurting people in the stands. He said the people in the stands no longer looked to the churches for help. They had become disillusioned with religion.

The Lord then said that the body of Christ would never make the impact upon the world that it should until they learned to work together instead of working against one another. God said that we are not competitors, but brothers and sisters working together to carry out His commandment and commission.

When Paul stood before Agrippa, he told them, "I was not disobedient unto the heavenly vision" (Acts 26:19). I do not want to be disobedient to the heavenly vision I experienced. Instead, I want to share what God gave to me so that it might find a place in the hearts of God-fearing, God-called men and women. We must be one in Christ, one in prayer, and, in cooperation, we must do the Lord's work.

CONTENTS

INTRODUCTION

AMERICA IS A NATION LOSING HER HERITAGE, losing her freedoms, losing her character, and, most of all, losing her favor with God. The message burning in my spirit is, "Awake, America," which became the title of this book.

I heard Hal Lindsey, a noted teacher on prophetic events, speak with Alan Bullock on *Celebration*, a program on Daystar Television Network, during the week of February 6 to 10, 2006. Lindsey said a ten-nation European federation will provide leadership to the world in the last days, but that he could not identify America anywhere on the global landscape.

Scott Dowlen, in an article titled "Does the Bible Tell the Future?" addressed this point by referencing Daniel: "Daniel spoke, saying, 'I saw in my vision by night, and behold, the four winds of heaven were stirring up the Great Sea. And four great beasts came up from the sea, each different from the other. The first was like a lion, and had eagle's wings.…And suddenly another beast, a second, like a bear.…After this I looked, and there was another, like a leopard.…After this I saw in the night visions, and behold, a fourth beast, dreadful and terrible, exceedingly strong. Those great beasts, which are four, are four kings which arise out of the earth' (Daniel 7:2–7, 17)." Dowlen believes that the lion is England, with the eagle's wings referring to the United States. He writes, "The lion had wings like eagle wings that were plucked off. Can that be said of England? Yes—the United States, whose symbol is the eagle, was initially a colonial branch of England which was 'plucked off' at the time of the Declaration of Independence and the following war for independence. This is the only part of scripture that I am currently willing to say contains reference to America—and note that the nation is not mentioned anywhere else in this prophecy."[1]

He continues, "This part of the prophecy clearly shows the structure of the coming world-wide government. A ten-nation union will oversee a governmental system that will eventually control most of the peoples of the world. Three of the ten original leaders will be overthrown in some way just as a charismatic leader emerges to fill the void. Many events in the world today point to a growing world government. The United Nations, the World Court, World Health Organization, World Trade Organization, and other 'global governance' entities are already in place. They are already ignoring the sovereignty of nations and exercising control over many weaker nations. All that remains to be seen is the ten-nation group that will unify to administer this system."[2]

Irvin Baxter Jr. of Endtime Ministries, has also said many times on his national radio show and on the Trinity Broadcasting Network that America cannot be identified in biblical prophecy during the End Times.[3]

On the other hand, many prophecy preachers believe that America will experience a great revival in the last days and that America will be the hiding place for the remnant of Israel when the armies of the Antichrist and his federation of nations are slaughtering Israel. It may be that the future of America and her place in the End Times will depend upon the body of Christ in America. Will the body of Christ see a renewal of its fervor? Will America experience a revival that impacts every level of society? Or will she fall by the wayside and be swallowed up by the regime of the Antichrist?

Let us ask, then, will America be a super power after the coming of the Lord? If not, what will cause our nation to descend from its position as the most powerful nation on Earth to a nation that is difficult to find or impossible to identify in prophecy? A quote by Benjamin Franklin offers a possible answer to this question. He said that without God's concurring aid, "We ourselves shall become a Reproach and Bye-word down to future Ages."[4] If America turns her back on God's help, she will become a byword for offending God. We must beware, lest this be the reason so many prophetic scholars cannot identify America in prophecy.

Powerful forces are trying to make America like other nations. These forces are determined to rob this nation of freedom of religion, freedom of speech, Christian symbols, and Christian expressions in worship. A significant force assailing America's religious freedoms is the Supreme Court, which has come to resemble an oligarchic power. Militant forces, with the assistance of the courts, are removing any evidence of Christianity in public and government properties. The recent establishment of the Department of Homeland Security, which has unprecedented authority over civil liberties, and the recent passage of the Real ID Act—which mandates new regulations for a national identification system that could lay the electronic groundwork for the mark of the Beast—move us to the brink of a police state. All of these various forces are changing the face and character of America.

In the midst of the anti-God, anti-Jesus, anti-Christian activities taking place, most Americans appear unaware of them. Citizens are not aware of the freedoms we are losing regularly. Churches are not aware of the religious freedoms being lost at a frightening rate. They will elect the politicians that promise them the greater financial rewards regardless of the direction their leadership takes America. People are more interested in their bowl of pottage than they are in their birthright.[5]

In *America Is Too Young to Die*, Leonard Ravenhill said, "This is the day of arrogant iniquity. It struts and strides, it screams from the billboards, it flashes from the television tubes. In a day when crime and cruelty saturate the press and television news, the public thirst for more; it devours television mayhem, murder, and sadomasochism. This is the day when all that is vile, vulgar, vicious, vain, and virtueless gets the headlines; and millions of dollars are invested to see that this tide of moral scum does not decrease."[6] He continued, "The disparity between New Testament Christianity and today's sick Church in a dying world is a sorry sight. That the Church is sick few will dispute."[7]

Too many churches are concerned primarily about what is happening within the four walls of their own church facilities. They ignore what is happening in the courts, in the schools, and in the government.

There is a frightening parallel between the rise and fall of nations and empires of history and the conditions of America today. A common thread runs through the history of nations that appeared on the scene for a time and then faded away: they became complacent, taking their privileges and freedoms for granted and as entitlements. Although the outward structure appeared to be sound, the inner structure was decayed and deteriorating. The populace forgot their heritage and the heavy price paid for it, and they became guilty of self-indulgence and gratification, immorality, sexual perversion, weakness, and greed. They turned their backs on God.

The following description, which describes the progression of the world's greatest civilizations' from their zenith of power to their fall, is attributed to Alexander Tyler, an eighteenth century Scottish historian:

> From bondage to spiritual faith;
> From spiritual faith to great courage;
> From courage to liberty;
> From liberty to abundance;
> From abundance to complacency;
> From complacency to apathy;
> From apathy to dependence;
> From dependence back into bondage.[8]

According to William Federer, "The average age of the world's greatest civilizations from the beginning of history, has been about 200 years."[9] He argues that these countries have followed Tyler's progression.

How does this progression relate to America? America has gone from a nation that implored the God of heaven for protection and for divine providence—with our inception as an independent nation a little more than two hundred years ago—to a nation that is in the process of removing any evidence of God from the government, from schools, and from public properties.

When Ronald Reagan made his official announcement for the presidency in the New York Hilton in New York City on November 13, 1979, he quoted John Winthrop. In 1630,

Winthrop stood on the deck of the *Arbella* off the coast of Massachusetts and spoke to the little band of pilgrims: "We shall be a city upon a hill. The eyes of all people are upon us so that if we shall deal falsely with our God in this work we have undertaken and so cause Him to withdraw His present help from us, we shall be made a story and a byword throughout the world." Mr. Reagan then responded to Winthrop's warning with these words: "A troubled and afflicted mankind looks to us, pleading for us to keep our rendezvous with destiny; that we will uphold the principles of self-sacrifice, morality, and—above all—responsible liberty for every individual; that we will become that shining city on a hill."[10]

This book, *Awake, America!*, examines where we are today. Have we fallen victim to Winthrop's stern warning of being a "byword throughout the world"? Or are we keeping our "rendezvous with destiny" to become that "shining city on a hill"? The choice America makes, the course America follows, is up to us.

Chapter 1
A NATION UNDER SIEGE

On December 7, 1941, America was attacked at Pearl Harbor. President Franklin D. Roosevelt described that day as "a day which will live in infamy."[1]

On September 11, 2001, America suffered another attack. This time, the attack was not on an island in the Pacific, but rather in the very heart of American democracy. Through television, the attacks upon the Pentagon and the State Department in Washington, DC, and upon the World Trade Center in New York City were experienced in every living room, office break room, and classroom in America.

What we now refer to simply as "9/11" will be burned into the memory of all Americans as surely as is December 7, 1941. In 1941, a powerful enemy with bombs, guns, and ammunition destroyed American ships in a sneak attack as they were anchored in a harbor of Hawaii. Since that time, the executive and legislative branches of the United States have given priority to a strong defense. They promoted a state-of-the-art SDI (Strategic Defense Initiative) or "Star Wars" defense system. They issued daily reports of our country's Patriot antimissile system, knocking out the enemy's Scud missiles during the Persian Gulf War. We reveled in our superiority and took great satisfaction in the security we felt because of our strong military.[2]

Then on September 11, America was attacked on the doorsteps of the nerve center of our nation, leaving thousands dead. Terrorists hijacked four airplanes and used three of them in the attack upon key targets. That heinous event effectively shut down this great nation. Eighty-two thousand government offices across America were closed. Every airport in America was shut down and forty thousand flights were cancelled. Sports arenas were dark because all sporting events were cancelled.

What powerful enemy could have invaded New York City and Washington, DC? What mighty sophisticated weapons were employed to wreak such havoc upon America? How many soldiers comprised such a mighty army that they could bring such devastation to the steps of our nation's capital?

Experts estimate only eighteen to twenty people—armed only with knives—brought the nation to its knees. Yes, September 11 was not only a day of weeping and mourning over the great loss of life, but an important sign that our security is not in missiles and tanks and guns or bombers or ships alone. Fewer than two dozen people armed only with box cutters wreaked heavy destruction upon America and effectively shut down the way America functions—and forever changed America's way of life. Because of the tragedy of 9/11, the people of this nation no longer feel secure.

As a nation sat transfixed and horrified before their television sets and heard the reports of the lives lost, the people injured, and the millions of dollars of property destroyed, they heard commentators, elected officials, and others speak of prayer. The God who had been rejected by the courts, who had to look at the No Trespassing signs directed at Him that crisscrossed America, now heard the people praying and exhorting the rest of America to pray for divine help.

The architect and designer of the World Trade Center was reportedly quoted as saying that an airliner could not knock down one of the buildings because of the structure's integrity and the steel used to build it.[3] The boast is reminiscent of those surrounding the Titanic. Supposedly, the Titanic could not be sunk because of airtight compartments that were independent of each other in the structure of the ship. Yet on a cold, foggy night, the icy finger of an iceberg ripped through the side of the ship and it sank.

The Fall revealed man's propensity to believe that he is capable and independent of the need for God's help. The serpent tempted Adam and Eve by suggesting that God had forbidden them from eating of the tree of the knowledge of good and evil because it would make them self-sufficient. (See Genesis 3:4.) But just as the first couple came face-to-face with their vulnerability after the Fall, the actions of modern men and women continue to demonstrate the scope of our dependence upon Him. Was 9/11 an example of how America's rejection of God as its protector has made our nation vulnerable to attack?

Learning From History

The history of humankind chronicles the rise and fall of nations. Not one nation has survived its own greatness. In some cases, stronger nations rose up and defeated them in battle. In other cases, decadence, opulence, and moral and spiritual weakness destroyed the foundation of the nation or empire.

What can be learned from the fall of past civilizations and nations that parallel America today?

Modern-day Iraq is the birthplace of the world's first civilization, which gave to the world writing, math, the calendar, an agricultural system, and the wheel.[4] Think of the current situation in Iraq, then contrast that view with J. N. Postgate's description of Mesopotamia (present-day Iraq) as a center "from which literate civilization radiated."[5] Thousands of years later, Iraq neither stands as a leader in literature, mathematics, nor agriculture. Instead, it is one of the most troubled spots in the world. Far removed from its past grandeur, Iraq's government has been a despotic, totalitarian system that has brutalized its citizens.

China played an important role in the development of civilization. My wife, Kathy, and I had the privilege of traveling to Beijing and walking on top of the Great Wall of China. We observed the astounding architecture of that civilization of many centuries ago.

The Great Wall is more than four thousand miles long and was built over a period of two thousand years (from 400 B.C. to around A.D. 1600). At thirty-five feet (6.6 meters) high and almost as wide, five or six horses can stand abreast on the wall. It was built by a workforce of nearly one million slaves and conscripted laborers. Tens of thousands of workers died on the wall and were buried where they fell because of the cruelty of the overseers.

The purpose of the wall was to protect China from warring tribes. Yet after two thousand years of labor and the lives lost in its construction, the wall did not prevent the invasion of China by the Manchu. How? The wall was very high, very wide, and very strong; it seemed impregnable. Since they could not go over it or around it, the Manchu passed through a gate opened by the Chinese general![6] The Chinese had expended all their energies and resources on building the wall, but had ignored the character of the people who were keeping the gates. Can a nation long survive if the moral character of the people is destroyed?

China's folly is an example of Isaiah 56:10–11:

> His watchmen are blind, They are all ignorant; They are all dumb dogs, They cannot bark; Sleeping, lying down, loving to slumber. Yes, they are greedy dogs Which never have enough. And they are shepherds Who cannot understand; They all look to their own way, Every one for his gain, From his own territory.

The watchmen on the Great Wall of China were neither blind nor ignorant concerning the dangers, but their moral failure caused them to sell out their country and their own posterity.

In the rise and fall of nations there seems to be a common thread: decadence, immorality, apathy, and loss of character and willpower. The denial and rejection of God is another factor. If a nation is strong enough militarily to defeat its enemies, then greater vigilance should be given to the dangers from within.

Edward Gibbon said this about the rise and fall of the Roman Empire: "The story of its ruin is simple and obvious; and instead of inquiring *why* the Roman Empire was destroyed, we should rather be surprised that it had subsisted so long. The victorious legions, who, in distant wars, acquired the vices of strangers and mercenaries, first oppressed the freedom of the republic, and afterwards violated the majesty of the people."[7]

The Romans acquired the vices of the people they conquered, and also from the mercenaries that fought with them and against them. The first act that undermines the greatness of an empire is its *oppression of the freedom* of the people. This caused Rome to violate the majesty of the Roman nation. When the freedoms of the people are taken from them, the next step in the progression is the *violation of the personhood* of the people—their dignity, their self-worth, their self-respect, their morale, and their spirituality. According to Gibbon, the Roman Empire was guilty of both of these crimes against its own people.

Russia will only be used here as an example of people who didn't realize the extent of the threat of communism until it was too late. When communism took over Russia, the communists were in the minority. Fred Scharz writes, "The Bolsheviks did not have wide popular support [for the revolution]....Bolshevism thus came to power with a tiny minority of the people, but they established their terror, and Lenin became the ruthless lord and master of Russia." He claims "they seized power utilizing deception, established themselves by violence, and maintained their dictatorship by totally enslaving helpless people."[8] How can a minority take over the control of a nation? When the population is apathetic and unconcerned and ignores the warning signs of the dangers and threats to the will of the majority.

The major world powers that later made up the Allied forces failed to understand the unfolding events that would lead to World War II. When Adolph Hitler re-armed Germany in violation of the Versailles Treaty, recaptured the Rhineland, and invaded Poland, the British falsely assumed that they could avert another war by making concessions to appease Hitler. Following the Munich Conference in September 1938, British Prime Minister Neville Chamberlain read the agreement signed by Germany, France, Italy, and England and concluded by saying, "My good friends, for the second time in our history, a British Prime Minister has returned from Germany bringing peace with honour. I believe it is a peace for our time. Go home and get a nice, quiet sleep."[9]

Appeasement is never the answer to aggression. When the enemies of a nation, a state, a city, or community are allowed to establish their strongholds within that area, appeasement is not the appropriate response. Chamberlain will forever be identified with appeasement and failure to stand up to the global ambitions of Hitler.

Unlike some of the other nations and empires that collapsed because of internal weaknesses, Germany presents a portrait of a nation overextended by the lust for power and by the aggression of its leader, Adolph Hitler. Hitler underestimated the will and resolve of the nations—such as Great Britain and America—he opposed.

Unlike Chamberlain, Winston Churchill recognized and fought against the dangers facing his country. In his first speech as prime minister, he offered "nothing... but blood, toil, tears and sweat."[10] Before the Battle of Britain, he promised, "We shall defend our island, whatever the cost may be, we shall fight on the beaches, we shall fight on the landing grounds, we shall fight in the fields and in the streets, we shall fight in the hills; we shall never surrender."[11] In another speech, he challenged, "Let us therefore brace ourselves to our duties, and so bear ourselves that, if the British Empire and its Commonwealth last for a thousand years, men will say, '*This* was their finest hour.'"[12]

Churchill breathed his indomitable spirit into a nation under attack and communicated his fire, courage, will, and never-say-die attitude to the people of the Commonwealth. This was an example of a ruthless dictator (Hitler) trying to subdue an immovable object (Churchill) refusing to surrender.

Good people must never acquiesce to the godless who seek to destroy their freedoms, whether overtly through aggression, war, or terror; or covertly through deception, manipulation, and political encroachment. In every battle between those who sought to enslave and those who refused to be enslaved, freedom prevailed only in those situations where someone loved freedom more than life. Liberty is too precious to be bartered away or to bow before the power hungry who seek to enslave. What a contrast between Chamberlain's policy of appeasement and Churchill's iron-will determination never to surrender.

Today, America is at war, although a different type of war than we have ever fought. This is not a military war or a terrorist war. Instead, this is the most important war that anyone ever fights: a spiritual war. Sadly, too many in God's army have gone AWOL.

Will we, like ancient Rome, adopt every vice, eventually losing our very souls? Will we, like China, be undone from within? Will we, like Russia, allow a minority to impose its evil will over the majority? Will we, like Chamberlain's England, appease evil until the streets run with blood? Or will we fight, as did Churchill's England and America, exposing evil for its lies and lust, forcing evil to understand that godly character always defeats unholy aggression?

The cry must go forth throughout America to wake up. This war—this call to action, this alarm to cast off our apathy and rise from our slumber—is our clarion call to action.

Chapter 2
A FOUNDATION OF FREEDOM

A nation which does not remember what it was yesterday does not know what it is today.[1]

—Woodrow Wilson

THE GLORIES OF GREAT NATIONS, WORLD POWERS, and dynasties were followed by a dismal aftermath. Regardless of their power, a time came when the blazing sun of their glory turned into a flickering flame.

Why has history repeated itself over and over in the records of nations and empires? We learn from fallen nations, some of which are mere historical footnotes, that the failure of the people to act enables a few men and women to rob a nation of its treasures. Ultimately, responsibility rests with the people.

America's treasures are freedom of religion, freedom of speech, and God's divine favor, all of which are at risk. God has placed in the heart of humankind the desire to worship and to serve Him. Failure to do so is not the normal response, but is an unnatural response to God's desire for fellowship with humankind. He has also placed within the heart of humankind the desire to be free: free to worship, free to speak, free to enjoy God's favor. Although there are arenas of life that are open to negotiation and to possible compromise, freedom is not one of them.

What does America stand to lose? The words to "America the Beautiful" describe the physical beauty of our great nation.

O beautiful for spacious skies,
For amber waves of grain,
For purple mountain majesties
Above the fruited plain!
America! America!
God shed his grace on thee,
And crown thy good with brotherhood
From sea to shining sea!

America is beautiful in its mountains, plains, forests, deserts, rivers, lakes, big skies, and seashores. But the song also describes an aspect of its beauty that transcends geography: "God shed His grace on thee." Another verse of the song speaks to another kind of beauty that goes far beyond the American landscape.

O beautiful for pilgrim feet
Whose stern impassioned stress
A thoroughfare for freedom beat
Across the wilderness![2]

This beautiful nation upon which God has shed His grace was established as a freedom-loving nation. But the freedom established—guaranteed—was not just any freedom. It was freedom as viewed from a Christian perspective. The Declaration of Independence explicitly connects freedom with God.

> We hold theses truths to be self-evident, that all men are created equal, that they are endowed by their Creator with certain unalienable Rights, that among these are Life, Liberty and the pursuit of Happiness.[3]

Alexis de Tocqueville, nineteenth-century French political commentator, said, "The Americans combine the notions of Christianity and of liberty so intimately in their minds that it is impossible to make them conceive the one without the other."[4]

With great foresight, America's founders established a government that protected individual freedom. Author Larry Pahl argues that a strength of America "is undoubtedly her epochal constitutional government with its written commitment to nationally protect the sanctity of the individual conscience. This was a grand and unique advance in mankind's search for political freedom. For the first time in world history no pope was to regulate faith, no Caesar was to punish heresy, no monarch, royalty, king, or State was to dictate morality. 'There was to be no religious test... required as qualification to any office or public trust under the United States.' (Article 6, Section 3 of the U.S. Constitution.) The congress was forever prohibited from establishing any religion or 'prohibiting' the free exercise thereof (Amendment 1 of the U.S. Constitution.)."[5]

How did this legacy begin? How did it happen that America's founding fathers valued freedom and the rights of each person with such fervency that they were willing to lose everything in a war to establish this unique government? Let's go back even further in America's history, even to England's history, to search for our answer.

Henry VIII broke the union of the English church with Rome and created the Church of England. The Act of Supremacy (1534) acknowledged the king as the only supreme head of the Church of England on Earth.[6] Many religious groups emerged, though, including Separatists—who we know as the pilgrims—who believed the Church of England too corrupt to reform, and, fearing persecution, fled.[7]

The English Civil War, which began in 1642, was partially instigated by religious conflicts between church and state.[8] The effects were far-reaching—even King Charles I was beheaded—but following the war, "Restoration England quickly became a boisterous polar opposite of the dour [Oliver] Cromwell years: ribald and immoral, and especially gleeful in its suppression of the troublesome Puritans....The so-called Clarendon Code...effectively broke Puritan political power."[9] This religious persecution was one of the primary factors for the immigration of Puritans from England to the colonies of America.

The early settlers were motivated by the desire for freedom *to* worship rather than freedom *from* worship. They risked their lives and endured hardships in order to worship according to their beliefs, not according to the dictates of the Church of England.

Many argue today for separation of church and state. Nowhere in the Constitution is there a statement regarding the separation of church and state. However, the framers of the Constitution were very careful to include a provision in the document to protect the people of the young American nation from the persecution and tyranny they had suffered from the government in England. The First Amendment of the Constitution states that "Congress shall make no law respecting an establishment of religion, or prohibiting the free exercise thereof."[10] The intent of this so-called Establishment Clause, along with that of the other of the Ten Amendments, "was to restrict the powers of the national government—or more accurately, to ensure that the restraints on it were maintained as represented. Clearly the Bill of Rights was not meant to provide more authority to the federal government than it already possessed."[11] That is, the First Amendment does not separate the government from religion. It limits the government from interfering in matters of religion.[12]

The fear of the framers of the Constitution was that the leadership of the nation and the leadership of the church would become one and the same and would punish those who were not of the same denomination or doctrine. They had already experienced hardships at the hand of the Church of England that punished those who were not part of the state Church. They made it impossible for America to declare any denomination the national religion. The men who wrote the Constitution took great pains to protect citizens from persecution; harassment; mistreatment; or the loss of life, property, or personal freedoms by the state because of their religion. They were also careful to protect the church from a government making laws that would impinge upon the church's freedoms.[13]

The second phrase in the First Amendment reads, "Congress shall make no law . . . prohibiting the free exercise thereof." It is perhaps ironic that today the courts use the bogus argument of the separation of church and state—a misinterpretation of the establishment clause—as a cloak for their anti-Christian decisions and, in so doing, violate this "free exercise" provision of the same Amendment.

America stands to lose both our freedom of religion and our freedom of speech in part through the activities of Constitutional revisionists.

The framers of the Constitution viewed the Constitution as the bedrock of our judicial system. But in recent years, too many judges seem to view it more as a rubber band that can be stretched in any direction and into any shape or form to fit their own agenda. It has been, at various times, the square peg and, at other times, the round hole. While the First Amendment speaks with clarity, these judges reinterpret and reinvent its meaning and intent.

When the New York Board of Regents attempted to compose a universal prayer that would not be offensive to anyone, they met unexpected opposition from the Courts. The prayer is quite simple: "Almighty God, we acknowledge our dependence upon Thee, and we beg Thy blessings upon us, our parents, our teachers and our Country." But the Supreme Court ruled it unconstitutional in *Engel v. Vitale* in 1962.[14]

According to David Limbaugh, "That *Engel* is now the law of the land doesn't alter the fact that many still believe that the Supreme Court wrongly decided it in the first place, based on its misreading of the Constitution and American history. Nothing better highlights this than reference to the learned rulings of the lower New York Courts in that case, all of which found the prayer constitutional."[15]

Justice Potter Stewart wrote in his dissent against the decision, "To treat a simple prayer the same as the establishment and patronage of a church by the federal government makes a mockery of the dangers the First Amendment aimed at preventing."[16] He declared that this ruling of the Supreme

Court was an example of what the First Amendment wanted to prevent from happening. This was why the First Amendment was put in place to begin with: to keep the Court from abusing religious freedom in America.

Justice Stewart continued, "For a compulsory state educational system so structures a child's life that if religious exercises are held to be an impermissible activity in schools, religion is placed at an artificial and state-created disadvantage. Viewed in this light, permission of such exercise for those who want them is necessary if the schools are truly to be neutral in the matter of religion."[17]

This is a powerful statement that makes several points:

1. The state requires a child to attend school.

2. The school influences the structure of a child's life.

3. Therefore, banning religion from the school biases the child *against* religion. That is, the child's attitude and values are impacted negatively toward religion because the school's position is that it is illegal to pray or read the Bible.

4. The only way for government to be neutral is to allow religious exercises for those who desire it, and not require it for those who are against it.

George Goldberg notes that, "Of the first thirteen judges who considered the constitutionality of the Regent's Prayer, among whom were some of the most learned appellate judges in the nation, eleven found it valid...and some of them felt strongly that any other decision would be historically wrong and itself constitutionally objectionable."[18]

The chief judge of the New York Court of Appeals (the highest state court) wrote, "Not only is this prayer not a violation of the First Amendment...but holding that it is such a violation would be in defiance of all American history, and such a holding would destroy a part of the essential foundation of the American governmental structure."[19]

Another judge on the New York Court of Appeals wrote in his concurring opinion, "It is not mere neutrality to prevent voluntary prayer to a Creator; it is an interference by the Courts, contrary to *the plain language of the Constitution*, on the side of those who oppose religion" (emphasis added).[20]

That prayer in school is unconstitutional was an opinion held by the minority of judges who first studied the New York Board of Regents' prayer. The Supreme Court's incorrect ruling has led to the contemporary—but similarly wrong-headed—view of separation of church and state. Although inherent in the Constitution is a separation in the sense that the state must not establish religion, nowhere does it explicitly address separation. Rather, the Constitution prohibits the government from interfering with the free exercise of the worship of its citizens. This point will be addressed at various times in this book.

Bernard Siegan argues that in the early days of our nation, "Neither (House or Senate) sought to eliminate all federal sponsorship of religious activity. The House rejected a provision that it had initially adopted requiring that Congress shall make no law 'touching religion.' In the very week that it approved the establishment clause, Congress enacted legislation providing for paid chaplains for the House and Senate."[21] Clearly, the framers of the Constitution did not intend for the federal government to eliminate religion from the public domain—even the government-sponsored domain—but, in fact, to *restrict the government from interfering with each citizen's right to act according to his or her religion.*

From its inception, America was a place of refuge, a place where the oppressed fled in order to avoid religious persecution and coercion. The early settlers paid a price for their newfound freedom. Some died crossing the Atlantic. Some died in the icy winters at Plymouth Rock and the other settlements of the New World. They faced hardships and challenges, but they persevered, survived, established colonies, and made the necessary adjustments to the new land.

When England placed restrictions upon the colonies of America similar to those that the citizens had suffered in the mother country, the new Americans rose up and threw off the yoke of England. Many died in the process, but they died to secure the freedom they so powerfully desired and so firmly believed to be granted by God to all humans.

Hear the words of Thomas Paine in *Common Sense*:

> But where says some is the king of America? I'll tell you Friend, he reigns above, and doth not make havoc of mankind like the Royal of Britain. Yet that we may not appear to be defective even in earthly honors, let a day be solemnly set apart for proclaiming the charter; let it be brought forth placed on the divine law, the word of God.[22]

Paine turned his attention directly to religion with these riveting words:

> As to religion, I hold it to be the indispensable duty of all government, to protect all conscientious professors thereof, and I know of no other business which government hath to do therewith.... For myself I fully and conscientiously believe, that it is the will of the Almighty, that there should be diversity of religious opinions among us: It affords a larger field for our Christian kindness. Were we all of one way of thinking, our religious dispositions would want matter for probation; and on this liberal principle, I look on the various denominations among us, to be like children of the same family, differing only, in what is called their Christian names.
>
> ...O ye that love mankind! Ye that dare oppose, not only the tyranny, but the tyrant, stand forth! Every spot of the old world is overrun with oppression. Freedom hath been hunted round the globe. Asia, and Africa, have long expelled her. Europe regards her like a stranger, and England hath given her warning to depart. O! receive the fugitive, and prepare in time an asylum for mankind.[23]

Those who first came to these shores sought freedom to worship according to their conscience. Those who secured America's freedom from England framed the Constitution with the intent to provide religious freedom and to protect all worshipers. Can we in good conscience watch in silence as the Constitution is distorted into its polar opposite? Can we sit in mute compliance as revisionists contort the Constitution into that which gives to the government power its framers forbade it to hold?

When we acknowledge that "God shed his grace on thee," we may ask, where are the "heroes proved in liberating strife who more than self their country loved and mercy more than life"?[24]

Chapter 3
GOD'S FAVOR UPON AMERICA

The settlers of the New World were primarily Christian. When America was first being colonized, the first building erected in any community was a church house, not a mosque or temple. One only needs to visit Jamestown, Virginia, to see the foundation[1] of the church where the government of the new nation met to conduct its business and to make wise decisions that determined the course and direction of this nation.[2] For over two hundred years, America has enjoyed the blessings, the protection, and the favor of God because it was established as a Christian nation. There are Muslim nations, Hindu nations, Buddhist nations, and more, but America was established upon the principles of Christianity with freedom of religion a fundamental right. This assertion does not argue for a Christian theocracy, does not recommend the establishment of Christianity as the state religion, and does not support the limitation of any religion. Instead, it does firmly point out that the principles upon which the United States was based were Christian principles.

The framers and signers of the Constitution were so concerned about freedom of speech and freedom of religion that they embedded into the Constitution that Congress would not make laws respecting a religion to compel or force people to adhere to a government-supported denomination, doctrine, or polity, nor to inhibit, restrict, impede, or prohibit the freedom of worship by any citizen.

We must heed the warning of Jedediah Morse, the father of American geography. In 1799 he said, "Whenever the pillars of Christianity shall be overthrown, our present republican forms of government, and all the blessings which flow from them, must fall with them."[3] In the previous chapter, I warned against the loss of our freedom of religion and freedom of speech. There is another treasure we stand to lose: the favor of almighty God! This divine blessing has been part of the essence of America since its founding.

But listen to the wise words of founding fathers and statesmen of our early history. Benjamin Rush, a signer of the Declaration of Independence, wrote in 1798, "[The] only foundation for a useful education in a republic is to be laid in religion. Without this there can be no virtue, and without virtue there can be no liberty, and liberty is the object and life of all republican governments."[4]

John Adams wrote in a letter to his cousin Zabdiel Adams on June 21, 1776, "[It] is Religion and Morality alone, which can establish the Principles upon which Freedom can securely stand. The only foundation of a free Constitution is pure Virtue."[5]

George Washington addressed the Synod of the Dutch Reformed Church in North America with these words, "While just government protects all in their religious rights, true religion affords to government its surest support."[6] Fisher Ames, Federalist Party leader, wrote in "An Oration on the Sublime Virtues of General George Washington": "Our liberty depends on our education, our laws and habits.... [It] is founded on morals and religion, whose authority reigns in the heart, and on the influence all these produce on public opinion, before that opinion governs rulers."[7]

While defending philosophers, Thomas Jefferson, in a letter to Edward Dowse dated April 19, 1803, wrote, "I concur with the author in considering the moral precepts of Jesus as more pure, correct, and sublime than those of ancient philosophers."[8]

Rufus King, a signer of the Constitution, included these words in a letter to C. Gore on February 17, 1820: "[The] law established by the Creator...extends over the whole globe, is everywhere, and at all times binding upon mankind."[9] Further, "[This] is the law of God, by which he makes his way known to man, and is paramount to all human control."[10]

The Constitution of the United States provides a model for every nation in the world that desires to be free, that desires to recognize the value and worth of every citizen, and that desires to provide and protect its citizenry from religious persecution. But today, activist judges, certain courts, and anti-Christian militant groups seem united to remove any symbol, expression, or record that America was ever a Christian nation. Christianity is under attack in America. It is absolutely necessary that the people of faith, the people of God, unite in prayer and at the ballot boxes to turn America back to God.

A Cloud of Witnesses

History is replete with the stories of people who stood against oppression and stood in favor of right. Hebrews 11—called the Hall of Faith—gives a brief history of people of faith who took such a stand. This Hall of Faith contains the names of people from every walk of life: kings and peasants; fearless leaders and followers; a great lawgiver and a harlot; warriors who subdued kingdoms and martyrs; people miraculously delivered from death and others who were tortured, stoned, and slain with the sword; those in palaces and those in caves. But each was a man or woman of faith "of whom the world was not worthy" (Heb. 11:38). Hebrews 12:1 refers to those faithful people of God who never allowed the rulers of their day to rob them of their freedom in God or of their faith as a great "cloud of witnesses."

This great cloud of witnesses was not only present in biblical days. American history also records a Hall of Fame and Faith. As the Declaration of Independence was being signed, Samuel Adams said, "We have this day restored the Sovereign to Whom alone men ought to be obedient. He reigns in heaven.... From the rising to the setting of the sun may his kingdom come."[11]

John Hancock, president of the Continental Congress, signed a resolution introduced by William Livingstone and printed in the 1776 *Journals of Congress* and in the Pennsylvania Gazette on March 20, 1776.

> In times of impending calamity and distress; when the liberties of America are imminently endangered by the secret machinations and open assaults of an insidious and vindictive administration, it becomes the indispensable duty of these hitherto free and happy colonies, with true penitence of heart, and the most reverent devotion, publickly to acknowledge the over ruling providence of God; to confess and deplore our offences against him; and to supplicate his interposition for averting the threatened danger, and prospering our strenuous efforts in the cause of freedom, virtue, and posterity.

> The Congress... Desirous... to have people of all ranks and degrees duly impressed with a solemn sense of God's super intending providence, and of their duty, devoutly to rely, in all their lawful enterprizes, on his aid and direction, Do earnestly recommend, that Friday, the Seventeenth day of May next, be observed by the said colonies as a day of humiliation, fasting, and prayer; that we may, with united hearts, confess and bewail our manifold sins and transgressions, and, by a sincere repentance and amendment of life, appease his righteous displeasure, and, through the merits and mediation of Jesus Christ, obtain his pardon and forgiveness; humbly imploring his assistance to frustrate the cruel purposes of our unnatural enemies; and by inclining their hearts to justice and benevolence, prevent the further effusion of kindred blood.[12]

In June of 1776, Abigail Adams wrote in a letter to her husband, John, "He who fed the Israelites in the wilderness, 'who clothes the lilies of the field, and feeds the young ravens when they cry,' will not forsake a people engaged in so righteous a cause, if we remember His loving kindness."[13]

Consider this admonition of General Washington: "Every officer and man will endeavor so to live and act as becomes a Christian soldier, defending the dearest rights and liberties of his country."[14] In his farewell speech as president on September 19, 1796, he said, "Of all the dispositions and habits that lead to political prosperity, Religion and morality are the indispensable supporters."[15] Found in George Washington's personal prayer book was this prayer: "Oh eternal and everlasting God...Direct my thoughts, words and work, wash away my sins in the immaculate blood of the lamb and purge my heart by thy holy spirit, from the dross of my natural corruption, that I may with more freedom of mind and liberty of will serve thee, the ever lasting God, in righteousness and holiness this day, and all the days of my life. Increase my faith in the sweet promises of the gospel....[Daily] frame me more and more into the likeness of thy son Jesus Christ, that living in thy fear, and dying in thy favor, I may in thy appointed time attain the resurrection of the just unto eternal life."[16]

John Adams, who followed Washington as president said in an address to military leaders, "We have no government armed with the power capable of contending with human passions unbridled by morality and religion....Our Constitution was made only for a moral and religious people. It is wholly inadequate to the government of any other."[17]

The next president, Thomas Jefferson, wrote on the front of his Bible, "I am a real Christian, that is to say, a disciple of the doctrines of Jesus. I have little doubt that our whole country will soon be rallied to the unity of our Creator and, I hope, to the pure doctrine of Jesus also."[18]

John Jay, the first Supreme Court Justice, said, "Providence has given to our people the choice of their rulers, and it is the duty, as well as the privilege and interest, of our Christian Nation to select and prefer Christians for their rulers."[19]

And pay heed to these words that have been attributed to Alexis de Tocqueville: "I sought for the key to the greatness and genius of America....Not until I went into the churches of America and heard her pulpits flame with righteousness did I understand the secret of her genius and power. America is great because America is good, and if America ever ceases to be good, America will cease to be great."[20]

Other non-Americans bore witness to this truth as well. England's Richard Price compared America to his own country in 1776 and concluded, "From one end of *North America* to the other, they are fasting and praying. But what are we doing?—Shocking thought! we are ridiculing them as *Fanatics*, and scoffing at religion—We are running wild after pleasure, and forgetting every thing serious and decent at *Masquerades*—We are gambling in gaming houses; trafficking in Burroughs; perjuring ourselves at Elections; and selling ourselves for places—Which side then is Providence likely to favour?"[21]

Such a cloud of witnesses can be found even in official American documents. Many state charters contain statements of allegiance to God and to Jesus Christ. The Fundamental Orders of Connecticut (1639), the first written constitution in America states, "The word of God requires that to mayntayne the peace and union of such a people there should be an orderly and decent Gouerment established according to God."[22]

In 1643, the New England Confederation wrote, "Whereas we all came into these parts of *America*, with one and the same end and ayme, namely, to advance the Kingdome of our Lord Jesus Christ, and to enjoy the liberties of the Gospel, in purity with peace."[23]

The Colonial Legislature of New York Colony passed the following in 1665: "It is ordered that a church shall be built in each parish, capable of holding two hundred persons; that ministers of every church shall preach every Sunday."[24]

The Rhode Island Charter (1683) clearly states, "We submit

our persons, lives, and estates unto our Lord Jesus Christ, the King of kings and Lord of lords and to all those perfect and most absolute laws of His given us in His Holy Word."[25]

In the Pennsylvania Charter of Privileges (1701) it is written that "all Persons who also profess to believe in *Jesus Christ*, the Savior of the world, shall be capable... [to] serve this Government in any Capacity."[26]

I agree with Thomas Jefferson that God is the author and provider of the liberties and freedoms we enjoy. Inscribed on the Jefferson Memorial are these words:

> God who gave us life gave us liberty. Can the liberties of a nation be secure when we have removed a conviction that these liberties are the gift of God?

My response is a resounding no. Our liberties cannot be secure when we remove the conviction that these liberties are God's gifts to America. Remember: the Constitution itself says that "all men are created equal, that they are endowed by their Creator with certain unalienable Rights." This means that our rights originate not with the Constitution, not with the words of men, not with the executive or legislative or judicial branches of government, but with God Himself! When we forget this, we endanger our liberties, for what man gives can be taken away; but what God gives is fundamentally, incontrovertibly, and eternally certain. Even the closing statement of the Declaration of Independence, which Congress unanimously ratified on July 4, 1776, reads, "And for the support of this Declaration, *with a firm reliance on the protection of Divine Providence*, we mutually pledge to each other our Lives, our Fortunes and our sacred Honor" (emphasis added).[27]

Patrick Henry, often referred to as the firebrand of the American Revolution, is remembered by his soul-stirring affirmation of freedom. We would do well to remember it and the rest of his speech, spoken on March 23, 1775, a moment when the outcome of the Revolutionary War was still in doubt.

> An appeal to arms and to the God of Hosts is all that is left us.... [We] shall not fight our battles alone. There is a just God who presides over the destinies of nations.... The battle, sir, is not to the strong alone.... Is life so dear, or peace so sweet, as to be purchased at the price of chains and slavery? Forbid it, Almighty God! I know not what course others may take; but as for me, give me liberty, or give me death![28]

If God gives us liberty, if God is the source of our rights, then how can we live deprived of that liberty and those rights? How can we grovel at the feet of men when God has declared us "heirs of God and joint heirs with Christ" (Rom. 8:17)?

America's Spiritual Heritage

In a letter dated January 8, 1799, Henry seemingly summed up the philosophy of the fifty-five signers of the Declaration when he said, "Virtue, morality, and religion. This is the armor, my friend, and this alone, that renders us invincible. These are the tactics we should study. If we lose these, we are conquered, fallen indeed.... [So] long as our manners and principles remain sound, there is no danger."[29]

When we lose our moral values, our virtue, and our faith in God, then we are no longer invincible. Henry said if we lose these, then we are conquered; but as long as we stay the course as first determined by our forefathers, then no danger exists.

Another quote attributed to Patrick Henry declares, "It cannot be emphasized too strongly or too often that this great nation was founded, not by religionists, but by Christians; not on religions, but on the gospel of Jesus Christ. For this very reason peoples of other faiths have been afforded asylum, prosperity, and freedom of worship here."[30] Is this not part of the genius of Christianity? It is because of the gospel of Jesus Christ that all religions enjoy freedom in this country, but when the Christian faith is placed in chains, all religions will suffer the same fate.

God is in the very foundation of America. This is demonstrated through the language and intent of the founding fathers, in the charters of the first states, and in our most precious documents. This religious foundation—which preserves freedom of religion and does not coerce religion—is one reason for God's favor upon this nation.

There are two countries where the divine favor of God is apparent from the beginning of their history. The first nation is Israel; this favor was first mentioned in Genesis 12 when God told Abraham that He had a designated place on this earth for him and for his posterity to occupy and live. It would be their land forever. Ten times God tells Abraham the land was his forever. God deeded the land to Israel and notarized it in heaven. God inserted a beautiful survivor's clause in the deed; Abraham's seed would never have to probate the will because the land belonged to them forever.

Further, God explained that not only would He bless them, He would also bless the people who would bless Israel. Israel is thousands of years old and the favor of God has covered Israel like an umbrella.

America is a young nation of just over two hundred years, but it is the second divinely favored nation. America is blessed and favored by God for many reasons. As already mentioned, the United States was founded and established by Christians as a Christian nation. The Bible was the foundation of its laws of justice, the main textbook of its educational curriculum, and the frame of reference for all other textbooks.

Throughout American history, leaders have incorporated God and religion into the fabric of American life. In 1777, the Continental Congress voted to purchase twenty thousand copies of the Bible for the people of this nation.[31] In 1863, Salmon P. Chase, then Secretary of the Treasury and later Chief Justice of the Supreme Court, wrote, "No nation can be strong except in the strength of God, or safe except in His defense. The trust of our people in God should be declared on our national coins."[32] The Act of 1873 approved by law the motto "In God We Trust" to be inscribed on certain coins (although the motto had been used on coins prior to this statute).[33]

The Pledge of Allegiance, written in 1892, was first used in public schools that same year. "Under God" was added to the Pledge by Congress in 1954.[34] While signing this resolution into law, President Dwight Eisenhower said, "In this way we are affirming the transcendence of religious faith in America's heritage and future; in this way we shall constantly strengthen those spiritual weapons which forever will be our country's most powerful resource in peace and war."[35]

One of the most important reasons for God's divine favor upon America is because she is an ally and defender of Israel. Such support has been given because of moral reasons and because of "military, political, and economic" reasons.[36] This support is also religious, at least for many Christians in the U.S. Michael McGarry explains that "support for Israel finds different bases. Some, especially evangelicals and fundamentalists, view the Jewish return to Israel as partial fulfillment of the prophecies of the end time. Others see the State of Israel as a just world response to what happened to the Jews in the Holocaust. Still others...support it as a faith and political commitment to their belief in a God who does not renege on his promises."[37]

When U.S. leadership has strayed from its support, American Christians have rallied to Israel's support. When President Jimmy Carter attempted to pressure Israel to "unilateral concessions towards Egypt and the Palestinians without first securing from the other side [the various Arab nations] any commitment to recognize the State of Israel,"[38] Christians pressed the issue. Prominent evangelicals, including W. A. Criswell, Hudson T. Armerding, Harold Lindsell, and John Walvoord, placed a full-page ad in *The New York Times* on November 1, 1977, that said:

> We the undersigned Evangelical Christians affirm our belief in the right of Israel to exist as a free and independent nation and in this light we voice our grave apprehension concerning the recent direction of American foreign policy vis-à-vis the Middle East. We are particularly troubled by the erosion of American governmental support for Israel evident in the joint US-USSR statement.

> "The time has come for Evangelical Christians to affirm their belief in biblical prophecy and Israel's Divine Right to the Land by speaking now."[39]

For whatever reasons, America has served as a brotherly protector to Israel, although both America and Israel receive their protection from God Himself. Benjamin Franklin explains that "in the beginning of the Contest with Britain, when we were sensible of Danger, we had daily Prayers in this Room for the Divine Protection. Our Prayers, Sir, were heard—and they were graciously answered. All of us, who were engag'd in the Struggle, must have observed frequent Instances of a superintending Providence in our Favor."[40]

Because our moral laws and principles are based upon Scripture, America has enjoyed an umbrella of God's blessings and protection. This is a critical point in understanding God's favor upon America. Although not American, many Americans would agree with John Locke: "The Bible is one of the greatest blessings bestowed by God on the children of men. It has God for its author; salvation for its end, and truth without any mixture for its matter."[41]

Horace Greeley said, "It is impossible to enslave mentally or socially a Bible reading people. The principles of the Bible are the groundwork of human freedom."[42]

As superintendent of schools in Washington, DC, Thomas Jefferson declared the Bible to be the primary text for teaching reading to public school students. In 1782, the United States Congress voted this resolution: "The Congress of the United States recommends and approves the Holy Bible for use in all schools."[43] If the people who wrote the Declaration of Independence passed a resolution that the Bible would be used in all public schools, then why would the Supreme

Court today rule that it is unconstitutional to pray or read the Bible in our schools?

Upon hearing a man defaming God's Word, Andrew Jackson, the nation's seventh president, rebuked him with the following well-chosen words: "That book is the Rockbed of the Republic."[44]

President Lincoln called William Holmes McGuffey, who wrote the *McGuffey Reader*, used for more than one hundred years in our public schools, the Schoolmaster of the Nation.[45] Mr. McGuffey said, "The Christian religion is the religion of our country. From it are derived our notions on the character of God, the great moral Governor of the universe. On its doctrines are founded the peculiarities of our free institutions. From no source has the author drawn more conspicuously than from the sacred Scriptures. From all these extracts from the Bible I make no apology."[46]

Ulysses S. Grant, the eighteenth president, said regarding the Bible, "To the influence of this book we are indebted for all the progress made in true civilization, and to this we must look as our guide for the future."[47]

Grover Cleveland, the twenty-second and twenty-fourth president, said, "All must admit that the reception of the teachings of Christ result in the purest patriotism, in the most scrupulous fidelity to public trust, and in the best type of citizenship."[48]

Former President Herbert Hoover, Mrs. Calvin Coolidge, Mrs. Theodore Roosevelt, Mrs. William H. Taft, Mrs. Benjamin Harrison, Mrs. Grover Cleveland, and others, in calling America back to their Christian heritage, issued the following joint statement: "Democracy is the outgrowth of the religious convictions of the sacredness of every human life. On the religious side, its highest embodiment is The Bible; on the political side, the Constitution."[49]

Harry S. Truman said, "The fundamental basis of this nation's laws was given to Moses on the Mount. The fundamental basis of our Bill of Rights comes from the teachings we get from Exodus and Saint Matthew, from Isaiah and Saint Paul. I don't think we emphasize that enough these days. If we don't have a proper fundamental moral background, we will finally end up with a totalitarian government which does not believe in right for anybody except the State."[50]

Woodrow Wilson, the twenty-seventh president, said, "The Bible...is the one supreme source of revelation of the meaning of life, the nature of God and spiritual nature and needs of men....America was born a Christian nation."[51]

Noah Webster, author of the first American dictionary, wrote, "[Our] citizens should early understand that the genuine source of correct republican principles is the Bible, particularly the New Testament or the Christian religion."[52] Calvin Coolidge summed American dependence on the Bible very well: "The foundations of our society and our government rest so much on the teachings of the Bible that it would be difficult to support them if faith in these teachings would cease to be practically universal in our country."[53]

Yet in *Abington School District v. Schempp* (1963), the Supreme Court ruled that Bible reading in the public school system violated the Constitution, although the Bible was quoted heavily by those who wrote our Constitution and shaped our nation, its system of education, justice, and government. In Lutz and Hyneman's study of more than fifteen thousand quotes from the founding fathers, they report that 34 percent of all quotes were directly from the Bible.[54]

James Madison, the fourth president and the primary author of the Constitution of the United States, said, "We have staked the future of all our political constitutions upon the capacity of each of ourselves to govern ourselves according to the moral principles of the Ten Commandments."[55]

How can the Supreme Court rescind all of the laws of this country that are based upon the Bible and Judeo-Christian teachings without dismantling the very structure of our government? The very structure of our government is based upon the Bible. Is the Supreme Court, with its misinterpretations of the Constitution and the war it wages against the Bible, destroying the very foundation upon which the laws of this country were founded? Were these justices not sworn to uphold the Constitution?

At the Constitutional Convention of 1787, James Madison proposed a plan to divide the central government into three branches. Some speculate that he discovered the model of government from God, the perfect governor, as he read Isaiah 33:22, "For the LORD is our Judge, the LORD is our Lawgiver, the LORD is our King; He will save us." In other words, the prophet is saying that the Lord represented the judicial, legislative, and executive head over Israel.[56]

The Court, and all Americans, should read and understand the psalmist: "Blessed is the nation whose God is the LORD." (Ps. 33:12). God blesses the nations that honor Him. The rest of the verse states, "The people He has chosen as His own inheritance." America's faith in God is declared in the Pledge of Allegiance, which states that we are "one nation under God" in recognition of our divine Benefactor. America wrote its faith and trust in God on its currency: "In God we trust."

Not only is Scripture engrained in the heart and soul of America, but so is prayer. Congress opens every session with prayer and implores divine guidance.[57] At a difficult and divisive time in Congress, Benjamin Franklin addressed the body:

> I have lived, Sir, a long time, and the longer I live, the more convincing proofs I see of this truth that God governs in the Affairs of men. And if a Sparrow cannot fall to the Ground without his Notice, is it probable that an Empire can rise without his Aid? We have been assured, Sir, in the Sacred Writings, that "except the Lord build the House, they labour in vain that build it." I firmly believe this; and I also believe, that, without his concurring Aid, we shall succeed in this political Building no better than the Builders of Babel; we shall be divided by our little, partial, local interests, our Projects will be confounded, and we ourselves shall become a Reproach and Bye-word down to future Ages. And, what is worse, Mankind may hereafter, from this unfortunate Instance, despair of establishing Government by human Wisdom, and leave it to Chance, War, and conquest.
>
> I therefore beg leave to move, That henceforth Prayers imploring the Assistance of Heaven and its blessing on our Deliberations, be held in this Assembly every morning before we proceed to business.[58]

Benjamin Franklin recognized God as the Governor and Blesser of this nation.

In his inaugural address, Washington felt the weight of his new office and appealed to God.

> Such being the impressions under which I have, in obedience to the public summons, repaired to the present station, it would be peculiarly improper to omit, in this first official act, my fervent supplications to that Almighty Being who rules over the universe, who presides in the councils of nations and whose providential aide can supply every human defect, that His benediction may consecrate to the liberties and happiness of the people of the United States a Government instituted by themselves for these essential purposes; and may enable every instrument employed in its administration to execute with success, the functions allotted to his charge.[59]

Senate Chaplain Peter Marshall prayed the following to open the June 27, 1947, session of Congress: "When we wait upon Thee, we shall not be shamed, but shall renew our strength. May we be willing to stop our feverish activities and listen to what Thou hast to say, that our prayers shall not be the sending of night letters, but conversations with God. This we ask in Jesus' name."[60]

Prayer, the Bible, and faith in God have been at the heart of the American experience since its beginning.

John Quincy Adams beautifully tied the birth of America to the birth of the Lord Jesus Christ when he delivered a Fourth of July speech at Newburyport, Massachusetts, in 1837:

> Why is it that, next to the birth of the Savior of the World, your most joyous and most venerated festival returns on this day? Is it not that, in the chain of human events, the birthday of the nation is indissolubly linked with the birth of the Savior?...That it forms a leading event in the progress of the gospel dispensation? Is it not that the Declaration of Independence first organized the social compact on the foundation of the Redeemer's mission on earth? That it laid the corner stone of human government upon the first precepts of Christianity?[61]

I will remark time and again in this book—because it cannot be emphasized enough—that America is a nation with divine favor because the prayers of her citizens, their faith in God, and their reliance upon the Bible have served as the bedrock and foundation of this country over our entire history. These prayers, this faith, and this reliance provide the backdrop for who and what we are as a people and as a nation.

America has been blessed and has enjoyed God's favor by having Christian leaders lead this nation in the most critical times of her history. I have already addressed the fact that the first president, George Washington, was a devout Christian. During the most tumultuous time in our history, America again was blessed to have Abraham Lincoln, who looked to God for guidance. Lincoln said, "I have been driven many times upon my knees by the overwhelming conviction that I had nowhere else to go. My own wisdom and that of all about me seemed insufficient for that day."[62]

Not only did God give Lincoln the wisdom to preserve the Union, but also to liberate the disenfranchised. God has always had a man in the presidency to provide leadership for the country in the most critical periods of history.

The recognition of a superintending Providence, a higher Power, a Creator, a divine Protector, a benevolent God—many names referring to the same person, Jehovah God—has been constant throughout the history of our nation up to this present day. I do not know of a time in history when an American president did not acknowledge the existence of God and His intervention in the affairs of humankind.

Former Chief Justice of the Supreme Court Earl Warren was quoted by *Time* magazine in 1954 as saying, "I like to believe we are living today in the spirit of the Christian religion. I like also to believe that as long as we do so, no great harm can come to our country."[63]

On January 25, 1984, Ronald Reagan said in an address to a joint session of the Congress on the State of the Union, "America was founded by people who believed that God was their rock of safety. He is ours. I recognize we must be cautious in claiming that God is on our side, but I think it's all right to keep asking if we're on His side."[64]

God has not only liberated and protected America, but has made her a liberator and protector to the weak and vulnerable nations of the world. As God has blessed America, she has in turn been a generous benefactor to the world. Reagan helped engineer the collapse of the atheistic Soviet Union.[65] Paul Kengor connects Reagan's stalwart effort to his faith: "He took it upon himself to confront the Soviet empire, and the Marxist-Leninist ideal that motivated it, more forthrightly than any American leader before him. And he did so in fulfillment of a role he believed God had assigned to America."[66]

Our military has been a protector to the global community. Our armies have patrolled a world in conflict. Our navy has sailed the high seas to keep the oceans free from tyranny. Our air force fills the skies to keep a vigilant watch over freedom-loving people. However, our strength is not in our military, but in the One who watches over us and who, I believe, brought America to her place of destiny.

Why has America assumed this mantle of tremendous responsibility? Because, at least in part, Americans have believed in a destiny linked to our moral virtue, the favor of God intertwined with our character founded upon God, faith, and Scripture.

Samuel Adams, the father of the American Revolution, said, "A general Dissolution of Principles and Manners will more surely overthrow the Liberties of America than the whole Force of the Common Enemy. While the People are virtuous they cannot be subdued; But when once they lose their Virtue they will be ready to surrender their Liberties to the first external or *internal* Invader.... If Virtue and Knowledge are diffused among the People, they will never be enslavd [sic]. This will be their great Security."[67]

Charles Carroll, signer of the Declaration of Independence, said, "Without morals a republic cannot subsist any length of time; they therefore who are decrying the Christian religion, whose morality is so sublime and pure... are undermining the solid foundation of morals, the best security for the duration of free government."[68]

Gouverneur Morris headed the Committee of Style, which prepared the final draft of the Constitution, and addressed the Constitutional Convention 173 times, more than any other delegate. He wrote, "Religion is the only solid basis of good morals; therefore education should teach the precepts of religion, and the duties of man toward God."[69]

Franklin Pierce said in his inaugural address on March 4, 1853, "It must be felt that there is no national security but in the nation's humble, acknowledged dependence upon God and His overruling providence."[70] Rutherford B. Hayes echoed similar thoughts in his own inaugural address years later on March 5, 1877: "Looking for the guidance of that Divine Hand by which the destinies of nations and individuals are shaped."[71]

I know that some who read this book will ascribe to me a provincial, rose-colored view of American history. No, I see the ugliness that has marred parts of our landscape. I understand that some politicians have pandered to American faith while seeking their own glory. I know that slavery blighted our nation for many years and that racism exists even today. I see the daily struggle of countless Americans. But I also believe that these—while elements within the tapestry that is America—do not represent the American core. The bad exists, but the good overwhelms it. Foolishness arises, but wisdom prevails. Greed, covetousness, and the seeking of power motivate many, but humble integrity has more often marked the character of those who bear responsibility for our nation's course.

I truly believe that America and its citizens are benevolent. America is a caring, generous nation whose citizens have opened their hearts and pocketbooks to help the starving, the sick, and the weak of the earth. Christian principles of justice for the mistreated, help for the helpless, assistance for the under-privileged, and protection for the weak, have inspired America to open her arms to receive people of all faiths and religions to be generous to the undeveloped and under-privileged nations, and to rush to the aid of the oppressed nations when they fall victim to the tyranny of the power-hungry nations of the world. The blood of Americans soaks continents around the world. American cemeteries dot the landscape of many of these countries. Though many accusations have been made to the contrary, America has never been afflicted with the disease of imperialism. We liberate rather than subjugate, support rather than dominate, protect rather than exploit.

Surely, the canker in the souls of other nations—those that have lost their resolve to be free and lost their dedication to freedom—will never afflict America when an overwhelming majority of its citizens believes in God. But is this still true of our country?

Chapter 4
A NATION AT RISK

Our destruction, should it come at all, will be from... the inattention of the people to the concerns of their country, from their carelessness and negligence, I must confess that I do apprehend some danger.[1]

—Daniel Webster

AMERICANS ARE A STRONG, COURAGEOUS PEOPLE who guard the truths that make this nation strong. The United States military is the best-equipped in the world.

But our nation is at risk.

This risk doesn't come from a stronger foreign power; instead, it is a familiar enemy, one that sits at our table and appears to be one of us. This enemy has already destroyed other nations that failed to recognize the warnings. It eroded the will and the moral fiber of those countries until the enemies were able to conquer by force, manipulation, subterfuge, compromise, or appeasement.

Cicero said:

> A nation can survive its fools, and even the ambitious. But it cannot survive treason from within.... For the traitor appears no traitor; he speaks in the accents familiar to his victims, and

> he wears their face and their garments, and he appeals to the baseness that lies deep in the hearts of all men. He rots the soul of a nation; he works secretly and unknown in the night to undermine the pillars of a city; he infects the body politic so that it can no longer resist. A murderer is less to be feared. The traitor is the carrier of the plague.[2]

Describing the face of Cicero's description of treachery, Thomas Jefferson said:

> From the conclusion of this war [for independence] we shall be going down hill. It will not then be necessary to resort every moment to the people for support. They will be forgotten, therefore, and their rights disregarded. They will forget themselves, but in the sole faculty of making money, and will never think of uniting to effect a due respect for their rights.[3]

What a true, sad statement and prophecy by Thomas Jefferson! The phrase—"and will never think of uniting to effect a due respect for their rights"—rings especially true. This is treachery in its most subtle form, disregard.

In *Whitney v. California*, Justice Lewis D. Brandeis wrote, "Those who won our independence believed that the final end of the State was to make man free to develop their faculties.... They valued liberty both as an end and as a means. They believed liberty to be the secret of happiness and courage to be the secret of liberty."[4]

Our enemy is different than those whom we have previously fought. This enemy is undetected, unrecognized, by the majority of Americans. With few exceptions, no outcry brings attention to this enemy. No warning calls the people to arms. Their tactics have not been barbed wire, guard dogs, tanks, artillery, or secret police. At least, not the literal versions. While we see no overt threat, the barbed wire is there. We hear no vicious guard dogs growling in the night, ready to devour, yet they are there. The ground does not rumble with tanks and artillery, and no secret police break down the doors to our homes under the cover of darkness to carry us away. Even so, their tactics steal our freedoms.

We know this enemy exists because we see the casualties of their aggression. We see their victims. Instead of America being, as Lincoln asserted, a "government of the people, by the people, for the people,"[5] the voice of the people is silent. Instead of the government being "the people's government, made for the people, made by the people, and answerable to the people,"[6] as Daniel Webster asserted, we have no adequate forum except in Congress and the ballot box.

The blood of the soldiers who have fallen in battle to gain our freedoms and to defend them, as well as the blood of our forefathers who carved this great nation out of a wilderness, cry out from the ground. We, the present generation, should applaud modern troops and the generations before us who paid such a terrible price for us to be free. We should honor the heroic gifts of their lives to us and for us, and we should stand up and shout, "Our forefathers and brothers did not die in vain!"

Benjamin Franklin said, "They who would give up on essential liberty for temporary security, deserve neither liberty or security."[7]

W. Somerset Maugham declared, "If a nation values anything more than freedom, it will lose its freedom; and the irony of it is that if it is comfort or money that it values more, it will lose that too."[8]

Jefferson agreed, saying that "all tyranny needs to gain a foothold is for people of good conscience to remain silent."[9]

We must not be the generation that lost these freedoms. We must not stand in the courts of heaven and be found guilty of negligence regarding the freedoms bought for us by such a monumental price.

The Casualties of Negligence

Where are the casualties, you ask?

Prayer in our schools is a casualty. The Ten Commandments that once adorned the walls of our schools and government buildings are casualties. Why do children carry guns to school and open fire on classmates and teachers seemingly without provocation? Some will say guns are the culprits. No! The culprits are the hearts of young people who no longer are exposed to prayer and who are no longer taught the Ten Commandments and the Word of God. They no longer possess the restraints from evil around them because of the removal of prayer and the Bible from their lives.

The rules that prohibit discipline in our schools and that fail to protect our school teachers from bodily harm have resulted in casualties.

The drug culture—rampant in our schools, playgrounds, and streets—destroys young lives by the scores.

Supreme Court rulings that sanction immorality and perversion as an acceptable lifestyle make morality a casualty.

Each of these losses is an injustice to the American people.

Without the principles of conduct to insulate our youth from the conflicting signals they receive at home, at school, and in the marketplace, they fall easy prey to the purveyors of filth, crime, and violence.

We should know that there is a price to enjoy the freedoms our forefathers secured for this nation. Christians understand that Jesus paid the price for freedom from the bondage of sin once and for all on Calvary, the price for our political and religious freedoms in this country must be paid again and again. The cost of maintaining freedom is the same discipline and vigilance as the price to gain them. Each generation must have a corresponding commitment equal to the previous generation to keep those freedoms secure. A nation that loses its freedom has typically done so because it forgot the price paid to gain it. Speaking of war's ability to cause citizens to recall the cost of their freedom, Jefferson once wrote, "God forbid, we should ever be twenty years without . . . a rebellion."[10]

John Adams also warned the country over two hundred years ago, "Remember, democracy never lasts long. It soon wastes, exhausts, and murders itself. There never was a democracy yet that did not commit suicide."[11] The key term here is *commit suicide.* America has stood strong against outside aggressors, but if America falls, the means will most likely be suicide, because free people, as in a democracy, too readily take freedom for granted. Citizens fail to exercise their freedoms and privileges, fail to go to the polls and vote, fail to resist the status quo even when freedoms are threatened. The question that faces us is whether we are nearing the time of which John Adams spoke.

The Fight for Freedom

In a forty-day span, 110,000 Marines on 880 ships sailed from Hawaii to Iwo Jima to engage the enemy. What awaited them? Twenty-one thousand Japanese, buried within the volcanic rock of the island. Today, the famous photograph of six American marines raising the flag on Mount Suribachi serves as an icon of perseverance and sacrifice against those who sought to rip from the world its freedom. (That image has been further immortalized in a statue that stands at the United States Marine Corps Memorial in Washington, DC.)

Shortly after the picture was taken on February 23, 1945, three of the six men were killed: Sergeant Mike Strank led his men up the hill, but was hit by a mortar on March 1, 1945. Harlon Block led the unit when Sgt. Strank was killed. His leadership lasted only a few hours; he was hit by a mortar the same day as his sergeant. Franklin Sousley was the third man to give his life.

John Bradley, one of the flag raisers who survived Iwo Jima, was later wounded in his legs. In an interview after returning to the States, Bradley humbly stated, "People refer to us [the men in the famous picture] as heroes; I personally don't look at it that way."[12] He went on to explain that what he and the other men did was no more brave than the actions of the other servicemen fighting in the war; they were just in the right place at the right time, he said.

Seven thousand American boys gave their lives on Iwo Jima so we could be free from tyranny, persecution, ignorance, and poverty; so we could be free to vote, free to speak, free to serve God and attend any church we desire, and free to worship God according to the dictates of our own conscience. One of the tragedies of war is that many who paid the price for our freedoms never had the privilege of enjoying them. Some never returned, while others came back home changed forever due to physical injuries or the emotional and psychological toll of the horrors of war.

Inscribed in the base of the United States Marine Corps War Memorial are the words of Admiral Chester W. Nimitz: "Uncommon valor was a common virtue."[13] This World War II generation is now routinely called the greatest generation.[14]

But can we afford for there to be a single greatest generation? Don't we need future generations to be great, too?

The people who desecrate the flag and the freedoms the flag represents did not pay the price for freedom. Will we as free Americans allow the atheists, the secular humanists, the Islamic terrorists, or any group to ensnare us, return us to bondage, and rob us of freedoms purchased at such a price? I pray not. We would be desecrating the memories of all those who paid the price with their lives.

John Quincy Adams once said, "Posterity—you will never know how much it has cost my generation to preserve your freedom. I hope you will make good use of it."[15] What a statement!

Remember these words attributed to Jefferson: "The price of freedom is eternal vigilance."[16] Too many people believe they are entitled to freedom, to happiness, and to the good life without earning them or paying any price to maintain them. Each generation must pay a price in willpower, determination, resolve, and sacrifice to protect the freedoms won by former generations. Without proper maintenance, freedoms, like old buildings, deteriorate, decay, and fall to the ground.

Eisenhower said, "If you want total security, go to prison. There you're fed, clothed, given medical care and so on. The only thing lacking...is freedom."[17] Is this the security we seek today?

Four hundred years ago, men and women were willing to face dangers and hardships to settle a new world for the privilege of worshiping God freely. They paid a great price, but never paid the debt in full because no single generation can pay it. Each generation must pay that price or freedom is forfeited.

The following contains excepts and paraphrases from Captain Stephen R. Ellison, a military doctor specializing in emergency medicine in the emergency departments of the only two military level one trauma centers, both located in San Antonio, Texas. He shares a touching story regarding some of the unsung heroes of the ongoing war to maintain our freedom. Captain Ellison recounts a few of his many experiences with the now-elderly veterans of past wars that he was privileged to serve in their last days and the kind of people they were. As I got a picture of these great soldiers, I was filled with pride again regarding the brave Americans who have given all they had to give so we can be free today. Captain Ellison wrote:

> These experiences have revealed the incredible individuals I have had the honor of serving in a medical capacity, many on their last admission to the hospital.
>
> There was a frail, elderly woman who... [had] a number tattooed across her forearm. I touched it with one finger and looked into her eyes. She simply said, "Auschwitz"....

> [There was a] long-retired colonel who as a young USN officer had parachuted from his burning plane over a Pacific Island held by the Japanese....
>
> I was there the night MSG Roy Benavidez came through the emergency department for the last time....He was so sick he didn't know I was there. I'd read his Congressional Medal of Honor citation and wanted to shake his hand. He died a few days later.
>
> The gentleman who served with Merrill's Marauders, the survivor of the Baatan [sic] Death March, the survivor [of] Omaha Beach, the 101 year old World War I veteran, the former POW held in frozen North Korea, the former Special Forces medic now with non-operable liver cancer, the former Viet Nam Corps Commander—I remember these citizens. I may still groan when yet another ambulance comes in, but now I am much more aware of what an honor it is to serve these particular men and women.
>
> ...I see later generations that seems [sic] to be totally engrossed in abusing these same liberties won with such sacrifice....My experiences have solidified my belief that we are losing an incredible generation and this nation knows not what it is losing. Our uncaring government and ungrateful civilian populace should all take note. We should all remember that we must "Earn this."[18]

Dr. Ellison's concerns that later generations seem "to be totally engrossed in abusing these same liberties won with such sacrifice" are borne out in a recent poll of high school students. A two-year study, sponsored by the John S. and James L. Knight Foundation, found that nearly three-quarters of the 112,000 high school students surveyed took the First Amendment for granted.[19] It is a sad condition in our nation when First Amendment freedoms are no longer valued by the younger generation of America. Former generations were composed of God-fearing, Bible-believing, praying people who were willing to make sacrifices to ensure their posterity could and would enjoy the freedoms they held precious. But now their posterity is unwilling to protect and preserve, or even value, those freedoms.

The results of a recent survey should alarm and distress all Christians. The survey reported that "more than one-quarter of American adults have left the faith of their childhood for another religion or no religion at all.... One in four adults, ages eighteen to twenty-nine claim no affiliation with a religious institution."[20] This survey alone should motivate Christians everywhere to join hands in an unparalleled effort to bring revival and renewal to America. The question that begs to be answered is this: if, as the survey reveals, one in four adults under the age of thirty has no affiliation with a religious institution, where will the church be by the next generation, should Jesus tarry? When we fail to pay the price of our freedom, the next generation will suffer the consequences.

Elmer Davis wrote that "this will remain the land of the free only so long as it is the home of the brave."[21] The price of freedom has always been high and many Christians have paid it with their lives. While soldiers of other faith traditions have fought valiantly for our country, no atheists,

Muslims, Hindis, or Buddhists signed the Declaration of Independence.[22] It was predominately Christians at Valley Forge who crossed the Delaware on December 25, 1776, at ten o'clock at night with rags wrapped around their feet because they had no shoes. Those brave men suffered malnutrition and frostbite and left their bloody footprints in the snow, but they prevailed. They had a burning desire for their children to live in a free world.

My intent is not to denigrate the contributions of other religions to America. One of the signature features of America's greatness has been her inclusion of people of various cultures, religions, nationalities, and ethnicities. Muslims, Hindis, Buddhists, and those of other religions are free to worship according to their beliefs; atheists are free to choose never to worship God. Christians have sacrificed for that freedom, just as some American Muslims, Hindis, Buddhists, and atheists have fought to preserve the freedom Christians enjoy.

We should not be intimidated by those who seek to restrict Christian freedoms in this country. Some individuals in America have paid little for these freedoms, yet are offended by Christian expressions of worship, though these have been practiced since the first day of our nation's independence. Some of the offended fled countries where no religious tolerance existed. They may have experienced persecution firsthand, but now that they breathe the air of freedom in their new country, they wish to revoke the freedoms and privileges Christians in America have enjoyed for over two hundred years.

In recent years, groups of illegal immigrants have marched in protest of the actions of Congress, at times marching with the American flag turned upside-down or with the flag of their home country topping the American flag. It is frustrating that to speak against illegal immigration is equated with racism or bias against immigrants. For most Americans, this is simply not a fair judgment. Many Americans understand that this country was built by hard-working immigrants. All of us arrived from elsewhere, whether mere generations or centuries ago. But illegal immigrants have broken the law. They cut the line ahead of their brothers and sisters who applied for entry via lawful channels. Further, many seem to feel a sense of entitlement: because they are here—no matter the means—they believe they have every right to be here. And, as stated above, many seem to place their loyalty with their originating country or their ethnic background rather than with the country they now seek to call home.

Nonetheless, we are not required to look to citizens of other nations to find those who threaten America. Americans, seduced by the gods of this world and without regard for those who have sacrificed to secure our freedom, endanger their own nation. God indicted Israel of this in Jeremiah 2:11:

> Has a nation changed its gods, Which are not gods? But my people have changed their Glory For what does not profit.

God could ask the same question of America: has America begun to serve false gods? Have the people of this country changed their glory for that which does not profit? Scripture warns countries against turning from God. The psalmist writes, "The wicked shall be turned into hell, And all the nations that forget God" (Ps. 9:17).

Calvin Coolidge said, "A nation that forgets its defenders will be itself forgotten."[23] America has forgotten its defenders, those who crossed the Atlantic and landed on the shores at great sacrifice of lives; who fought against tyranny in the Revolutionary War when the colonies were outmanned, underfed, underclothed, and equipped with inferior weapons; who fought in the Civil War, brother against brother and father against son, to root out the insidious thought that one man can own another. God gave our nation freedom and national independence; who fought in World War I, preserving freedom by paying the price on foreign soil; who, in World War II, waged war against a madman with ambitions of ruling the world who tried to place chains and iron bracelets around the necks and ankles of a Christian nation.

Yes, America has forgotten what made her great. America has forgotten the primary factor in determining the outcome of all of its wars: God. Benjamin Franklin, referring to God, asked, "And have we now forgotten that powerful friend?"[24] Isaiah issued a stern warning that "the nation and kingdom which will not serve [God] shall perish, And those nations shall be utterly ruined" (Isa. 60:12).

On June 6, 1984, President Ronald Reagan was to visit France to mark the fortieth anniversary of D-Day. In preparing his commemorative speech, Reagan's speechwriter drew on a quote by journalist Lance Morrow: "The ceremonies in Normandy will celebrate the victory and mourn the dead. They will also mourn the moral clarity that has been lost, a sense of common purpose that has all but evaporated."[25]

What a powerful statement! "*They will also mourn the moral clarity that has been lost.*" Yes, when America lost her memory of God's favor and God's blessings, she also lost her moral clarity. What a confusing moral landscape youth of this nation face! When a people dishonor God, soon they dishonor one another. Instead of schools, churches, and homes, television now serves as the primary teacher of social mores and value systems for our youth. Humility, compassion, caring for one's neighbor, good citizenship, and Christian values are being replaced with marketing campaigns telling us that nice guys finish last; movies that glorify violence, drug use, and profanity; and sports "heroes" who seem to live by the slogan, "Humility and apology are signs of weakness." All of these reveal the narcissistic direction toward which America is traveling. Yes, moral clarity is lost. Good is thought evil; evil is promoted as good.

America has six prominent enemies that must be fought: secular humanism, activist judges, anti-Christian militant groups, federal government encroachment, anti-Israel political forces, and Christian apathy. In the following chapters, we will examine these enemies of American and Christian freedom.

Chapter 5
SECULAR HUMANISM

SECULAR HUMANISM IS NOW THE GOD OF AMERICA. What is secular humanism? Steve Bruce explains, "...Secular humanists believe in the removal of religion from the public arena, in the tolerance of alternative lifestyles, and in the extension of choice. But the sociologist of modernity sees the secular humanist position as little more than the intellectual endorsement of what has already come to pass."[1]

From a Christian perspective, secular humanism has been identified as "a religious worldview based on atheism, naturalism, evolution, and ethical relativism."[2] Secular humanists tend to deny that secular humanism is a religion. The Council for Secular Humanism identifies it in the following way:

> ...a way of thinking and living that aims to bring out the best in people so that all people can have the best in life. Secular humanists reject supernatural and authoritarian beliefs. They affirm that we must take responsibility for our own lives and the communities and world in which we live. Secular humanism emphasizes reason and scientific inquiry, individual freedom and responsibility, human values and compassion, and the need for tolerance and cooperation.[3]

The Council's Web site identifies twenty-one affirmations, which is more than many churches list in their statements of faith! Some of them are:

- We deplore efforts to denigrate human intelligence, to seek to explain the world in supernatural terms, and to look outside nature for salvation.

- We are committed to the principle of the separation of church and state.

- We are concerned with securing justice and fairness in society and with eliminating discrimination and intolerance.

- We affirm humanism as a realistic alternative to theologies of despair and ideologies of violence and as a source of rich personal significance and genuine satisfaction in the service to others.

It is interesting how dogmatic anti-dogmatists who disparage Christian dogmatism can be!

Whether or not the Council of Secular Humanism intends the same, in many instances in contemporary society *tolerance* means that all must be tolerated except traditional values or Christianity; *separation of church and state* means the establishment of secular humanism as the *de facto* religion; *ignorance* means anything faith-based or belief in the Bible; and the very idea of God (theology) leads to despair and violence.

It is not surprising that secular humanism does not fall within the purview of the First Amendment's establishment clause. The Council reports that, "To date, the concept of secular humanism as a religion under the establishment clause has not been accepted by the judiciary."[4] This enables secular humanism to be promoted within schools and other public venues with impunity. By divorcing secular humanism from the establishment clause and by teaching it exclusively, it enables the government to establish secular humanism without fear of censure or contradiction.

Yet early humanists precisely did consider humanism, including secular humanism, a religion. Consider Charles F. Potter's *Humanism: A New Religion*. Not only does he establish humanism as a religion, but he identifies a key tactic for spreading this religion: "Education is thus a most powerful ally of Humanism, and every American public school is a school of Humanism. What can the theistic Sunday-schools, meeting for an hour once a week, and teaching only a fraction of the children, do to stem the tide of a five-day program of humanistic teaching?"[5] The Humanist Manifesto of 1933 states that the "purpose and program of humanism" is "the intelligent evaluation, transformation, control, and direction of such associations and institutions with a view to the enhancement of human life."[6] By Humanist Manifesto III, the religious language had been toned down, but secular humanism is still identified as "a progressive philosophy of life."[7]

Are we really to believe that secular humanism is *not* a religion and that the government has *not* established it as the religion of the land? It seems that Christianity and the other religions are competing against secular humanism for the minds and souls of American children and that the Supreme Court and other courts have given secular humanists a huge advantage in our schools. Though more than 75 percent of Americans polled in a joint study by CNN, *USA Today*, and Gallup disapproved of the order to remove the monument from the courthouse rotunda,[8] the secular humanists continue to impose their agenda on this country.

Justice Potter Stewart, writing in *Abington School District v. Schempp,* was wise enough to recognize that "a refusal to permit religious exercises thus is seen, not as the realization of state neutrality, but rather as the establishment of a religion of secularism."[9] Justice Stewart states further, "If religious exercises are held to be an impermissible activity in schools, religion is placed in an artificial and state-created disadvantage.... And a refusal to permit religious exercises thus is seen, not as the realization of state neutrality, but rather as the establishment of a religion of secularism, or at least, as government support of the beliefs of those who think that religious exercises should be conducted only in private."[10]

No, the forefathers didn't declare it. The Constitution didn't mandate it. The Declaration of Independence doesn't address it. But the judicial system in America—pointedly ignoring the spirit and intent of those who paid the price to establish our freedom and win our independence as a free nation—has, by its actions, designated America as a non-Christian nation.

An example of this effort is the removal of Chief Justice Roy Moore of the Alabama Supreme Court from office in Montgomery, Alabama. Judge Moore lives in Montgomery only one hundred miles from where I lived for a number of years, and he was impeached because he refused to comply with a federal court mandate to remove the Ten Commandments from the rotunda of the courthouse where his office was at the time. In response to the action against him, Judge Moore said, "It is a sad day in our country when the moral foundation of our law and the acknowledgment of God has [sic] to be hidden from public view to appease a federal judge."[11]

Thomas Jefferson was right when he said, "No power over the freedom of religion [is] delegated to the United States by the Constitution."[12] Justice Hugo L. Black said, "The very reason for the First Amendment is to make the people of this country free to think, speak, write and worship as they wish, not as the Government commands."[13] There is much evidence to suggest that Justice Black was very much in favor of the separation of church and state, and it seems from this quote from his opinion in *International Association of Machinists v. Street* that he was advocating that people be free to worship, not just be free from worship.

Radio talk show host Chuck Baldwin attended the trial of Judge Roy Moore and described it as an "inquisition." He said that the judges who heard the chief justice's hearing refused to allow him to present evidentiary material and refused to allow his attorneys to call a number of witnesses, including former Alabama governor Fob James. Baldwin said, "There was never a doubt that the judges had made up their minds to remove Chief Justice Moore from the bench before the proceedings ever began. They sat like wooden Indians throughout the trial, taking few notes and, with only one exception, making no comments, and asking no questions."[14] We thought every citizen could be assured of a fair trail. Now, in too many cases, the agendas of the judges, rather than the law provided by the Constitution, prevail.

Who could have imagined a few years ago that the conditions we experience today would take place in America? We thought prayer in schools would never be outlawed; but it was. We thought it would never be a crime to place the Ten Commandments on the property of government buildings; but it is. We thought same-sex marriages would never be legalized; but, in some states, they are.

We also thought abortion would never be legalized, that Americans would never stand for the slaughter of unborn babies, and yet current abortion statistics in the U.S. are startling. Nearly 50 percent of pregnancies are unintended, 40 percent of which end in abortion. Of all U.S. pregnancies, 24 percent are terminated via abortion. An estimated forty-two million legal abortions were performed in the U.S. from 1973 through 2002,[15] with another 1,287,000 in 2003. (In that year, an estimated 2 percent of women aged 15 to 44 had an abortion).[16] At this rate, the number of abortions performed will reach fifty million in 2008.

Five days after the unthinkable attack upon the Twin Towers and World Trade Center, Representative Adam Schiff, a member of the Committee on International Relations, addressed the House of Representatives. He said, "We will not relinquish our freedoms of speech, assembly and religion, nor sacrifice our precious right of privacy or way of life."[17] This is indeed a powerful statement, if it were true. But actions speak louder than words, as the proverb attests. The actions of the judiciary branch and the legislature—as well as the inaction of Congress at key moments—make a mockery of Representative Schiff's words.

Donald E. Wildmon, founder and chairman of the American Family Association, reported the objection of Senator Mark Dayton to a constitutional amendment defining marriage as being between one man and one woman: "Showing complete intolerance for those who disagree with him, Senator Mark Dayton of Minnesota recently accused those opposing homosexual 'marriage' of spewing 'hatred and inhumanity'.... He said such an amendment is 'vicious, ugly, mean-spirited and should be illegal.'"[18] Through Senator Dayton's words and through many other examples we see one of the methods used by the secular humanists: intimidation. The people of God must not allow the rantings of those who would destroy the moral fiber and religious freedoms in America to intimidate or silence our witness. As the safeguards of our freedoms and liberties are challenged, we must be resolved to stand strong and firm.

Jefferson connected God to liberty: "The God who gave us life gave us liberty at the same time."[19] He said, further, "And can the liberties of a nation be thought secure when we have removed their only firm basis, a conviction in the minds of the people that these liberties are of the gift of God?"[20]

In the previous chapter, we addressed the forgetfulness of Americans. Franco-Czech writer Milan Kundera echoes this concern in this chilling warning: "The first step in liquidating a people is to erase its memory. Destroy its books, its culture, its history. Then have somebody write new books, manufacture a new culture, invent a new history. Before long the nation will begin to forget what it is and what it was."[21] The enemies of Christ and of freedom are in the process of erasing our memory and history, and of creating a new culture and lifestyle.

Many people see Canada's Bill C-250 as a threat against Christians who might speak or preach against homosexuality, even when quoting the Bible as their source. The amendment to the hate propaganda law, which already protected individuals from discrimination on the basis of such factors as race, religion, ethnicity, and color, increased the penalty for speaking against individuals on the basis of their sexual orientation.[22] Although one of the bill's "good faith" provisions includes an exception if a person's expression is based on a belief in a religious text, this could be nullified if the Bible were labeled propaganda. The protection afforded by the provision may be tenuous, at best, because it may be difficult to determine who is speaking in good faith.[23]

An article in *Christianity Today* reports a similar situation in Sweden, which in 2002 amended its Constitution to include homosexuals and transgendered individuals in its list of groups protected from "unfavorable speech." Later, a Swedish Pentecostal pastor was charged with inciting hatred after he preached against homosexuality. He was found guilty and sentenced to one month in prison.[24]

Even without the force of law, the Christian message is censored. According to a news report by Art Moore, San Antonio-based pastor John Hagee's television show was taken off the air in Canada because of complaints from Muslim viewers. Moore wrote, "An American evangelist's television series on Islam in America was canceled by a Canadian station after the first program because Muslims complained his tone and demeanor was [sic] an incitement of hatred. San Antonio-based pastor John Hagee's 'tone in his comparison of what Christians believe according to the Bible and what Muslims believe according to the Quran' violated the code of ethics of

Toronto station CTS, said Program Manager Rob Sheppard in a letter of apology to a Muslim activist group."

Moore quotes Sheppard as saying, "You could see what he was trying to do by his tone and body language." The article states, "It wasn't so much his exact words, Sheppard said, but Hagee's purported inference Muslims cannot be loyal Americans." The action by the station was taken because of fifty to one hundred viewer letters, primarily, according to Sheppard, from Muslims.[25] Were there not fifty Christians who protested the cancellation? If not, why? We live in a global community, and what happens to our neighbors can happen to us. Though still a minority, Muslims are vocal in America as well, but Christians are so silent that a few Muslims seem to exert greater influence upon many decisions made in America than do Christians.

Eleven Christians distributing literature and quoting verses from the Bible at Philadelphia's Outfest event in 2004 were jailed; five faced various charges, including criminal conspiracy, possession of instruments of crime (their Bibles), reckless endangerment of another person, ethnic intimidation, riot, failure to disperse, disorderly conduct, and obstructing highways. If convicted, these Christians faced forty-seven years in prison. Thankfully, Judge Paula Dembe ruled that the charges had no basis. Not long ago, it would have been inconceivable that the charges could have ever been brought in the first place.[26] The secular humanist agenda was once again exposed.

These are merely a few of the activities that demonstrate actions against Christians and Christian values. How are they tied to secular humanism? Again, read the affirmations of secular humanism listed at the beginning of this chapter.

The language sounds lofty, but the tactics to implement this ideology are chilling. Take the following affirmation: "We are committed to the application of reason and science to the understanding of the universe and to the solving of human problems."[27] This deification of human reason—the supplanting of God and God's Word with the human mind—leads to an intolerant denigration of faith-based belief systems. The humanist viewpoint that only reason and science can solve human problems is arrogant and is reflected in the disdain shown toward Christians. I believe I can learn from non-Christians, from philosophers, scientists, and other faiths. Naturally, I understand that what I learn from them is not divinely-rooted or inspired by the Bible, but I do not doubt that there is wisdom beyond my own understanding.

Humanists profess to "believe that scientific discovery and technology can contribute to the betterment of human life."[28] In itself, this latter affirmation is one I can myself make. Christians and non-Christians alike benefit from science and technology, but the difference is that I believe that all science was *created* by God and is subject to God. I also believe that the religion of science is dangerous, as it seeks to empower the courts, schools, and others to replace God with scientific theory and to reject any thought that is not consistent with scientific dogma.

Another humanist affirmation boldly declares, "We are committed to the principle of the separation of church and state."[29] As I have already addressed, the Constitution does not use the language of the separation of church and state. Rather, it prohibits the government from *establishing* religion. Anti-religion laws are, in effect, the establishment of a non-theistic religion. To affirm the separation of church and state is to seek to force religion out of all public venues, thereby limiting freedom of speech, limiting freedom of religion, and establishing secular humanism as the state ideology.

A fourth example: "We are concerned with securing justice and fairness in society and with eliminating discrimination and intolerance."[30] "Eliminating discrimination and intolerance" is often a euphemism for the suppression—if not the outlawing—of alternative viewpoints, particular Christian views. Again, eliminating intolerance often employs the tactic of violating free speech.

Secular humanists also profess to "respect the right to privacy. Mature adults should be allowed to fulfill their aspirations, to express their sexual preferences, to exercise reproductive freedom, to have access to comprehensive and informed health-care, and to die with dignity."[31] In that one affirmation, we find many liberal touchstones: homosexuality, abortion, healthcare, and euthanasia. Is it any wonder that same-sex marriage, abortion-on-demand, socialized medicine, and doctor-assisted suicide are prominent issues in today's political arena?

Proponents of end-based ethics rely on the situation with which they are confronted to determine the course of action, which results in a "system" of ethics that is changeable rather than constant. A consistently consequentialist ethic rejects a higher authority, such as the Bible, to determine what ought to be done. That is what is meant by the affirmation that "moral principles are tested by their consequences."[32]

These examples are not limited simply to ideology; they are the basis for actions that are limiting freedom of speech and religion and indoctrinating American children with humanistic beliefs every day. They are also a compelling indication that issues facing America today are not accidental, but are part of a larger plan by secular humanists, some of whom hold positions of great authority.

Chapter 6
ACTIVIST JUDGES

SOME OF THE MOST EFFECTIVE INSTRUMENTS USED by the secular humanist movement are the Supreme Court and activist judges on the lower courts. They have reinterpreted the Constitution through the lens of secular humanism, replacing traditional values and our Christian foundation with its own ideology. They ignore those founders who sacrificed their lives to create a nation where its citizens could serve God without harassment.

Hard-won freedoms are now at risk. Lieutenant Colonel Joseph H. Kress, now retired, wrote:

> Half of the Supreme Court justices are of the mind that the United States Constitution is a living document. The Soviet Union's Constitution paralleled much of what is in the U. S. Constitution, except that it could be changed to accommodate the exigencies of the moment. In other words, Soviet Courts interpreted a living constitution, which is in reality no constitution. Ignoring the wisdom of it drafters, the liberal members think of the Constitution as an anachronism that stifles change—a barrier to social fine-tuning. Although they won't admit it, their belief is that the Constitution should be viewed under glass—a historical memento, not the key foundation block of the Republic. These black-robed termites undermine

> the Republic's pilings by creating rather than interpreting the Constitution.[1]

Judges encroach on the rights of citizens in many ways. In *Kelo et al v. City of New London* (2005), the Supreme Court ruled that it is permissible for local governments to seize private property with appropriate compensation for private economic development if the outcome would benefit the public. Remember the consequentialist ethic noted in the previous chapter? Speaking against this practice of confiscating local property, Sandra Day O'Conner wrote that "the ruling favors the most powerful and influential in society and leaves small property owners little recourse." Historically, seizures were allowed only for purposes such as building schools or other public spaces. Now, economic development initiatives, including sports stadiums and shopping malls, are cropping up to steal private property for the "public good."[2]

In a 1950 Supreme Court case, Justice Robert H. Jackson recognized limitations of the Court, saying, "It is not the function of our government to keep the citizen from falling into error; it is the function of the citizen to keep the government from falling into error."[3] Sadly—and dangerously—activist judges have positioned themselves as arbiters of citizen activities, also establishing themselves as sole and final authority on executive and legislative action.

The courts rob state legislatures of their legal authority and usurp the authority of the United States Congress. In *Lawrence v. Texas*, the Supreme Court ruled that consensual, homosexual sex was a constitutionally-protected right. This ruling invalidated sodomy laws in a number of states.[4]

Dr. Thomas Abshier wrote about the consequences of the *Lawrence* ruling in a powerful communiqué: "The 'activist' judges have thrown the moral structure of the nation's legal system into turmoil by ruling that we must expunge laws which incorporate principles identifiable as originating from the Judea-Christian moral system."[5] He accuses these judges of expunging laws, not because of the question of their legality, but on the sole basis of whether or not they originated from the teachings of the Bible. Abshier continued:

> We cannot stand by as the judicially enforced Secularization of America is thrust upon us in the name of Constitutional intent. We will suffer an unacceptable societal degradation if we capitulate to the Secular Humanist dogma of 'Separation.' We must each participate in the larger effort to defend the Christian worldview as our judicial, legal, and cultural moral standard. We must abandon our false pacifistic notions of Christianity and speak the truth with love. We may offend those who oppose us, but if our words are True they will have power. We must use the minimum force necessary to repel the invaders in our defense of truth. Truth needs a voice, and she depends on us to speak for her."[6]

While spreading their secular humanist dogma, the courts have ignored the First Amendment of the Constitution. The government is not to prohibit or infringe upon the freedom of our worship. The government is not to make laws for the establishing of religion. Yet these are exactly what they have done; the Supreme Court and activist judges have established a religion—secular humanism—and have made laws to support it. Through the Supreme Court, secular humanism has taken over our schools, taken over government, seized properties, and invaded our homes. The courts have even expanded their jurisdiction to cover the manner in which parents teach and discipline their children. They have insinuated themselves—ironically, often, under a banner of privacy—into nearly every aspect of American life.

Was the Supreme Court intended by the founders to have this power? The answer is no! In an 1804 letter to Abigail Adams, President John Adams's wife, Thomas Jefferson wrote, "But the opinion which gives to the judges the right to decide what laws are Constitutional, and what not, not only for themselves in their own sphere of action, but for the Legislative and Executive also, in their spheres, would make the judiciary a despotic branch."[7] This issue still burned in him many years later. In a letter to William C. Jarvis in 1820, Jefferson addressed the issue again, saying, "You seem... to consider the judges as the ultimate arbiters of all constitutional questions; a very dangerous doctrine indeed, and one which would place us under the despotism of an oligarchy.... The Constitution has erected no such single tribunal, knowing that to whatever hands confided, with the corruption of time and party, its members would become despots."[8] Jefferson said to consider the judiciary as having sole authority to decide the constitutionality of a matter would place America under a despotic oligarchy. He then made the very powerful statement that the "Constitution has erected no such single tribunal." I repeat the earlier statement that the Supreme Court has usurped the authority of the legislative and executive branches of government.

In an October 31, 1823, letter to Monsieur A. Caray, Jefferson explains the founders' intent and the subsequent usurpation of that intent.

> At the establishment of our Constitutions, the judiciary bodies were supposed to be the most helpless and harmless members of the government. Experience, however, soon showed in what way they were to become the most dangerous; that the insufficiency of the means provided for their removal gave them a freehold and irresponsibility in office; that their decisions, seeming to concern individual suitors only, pass silent and unheeded by the public at large; that these decisions, nevertheless, become law by precedent, sapping, by little and little, the foundations of the constitution, and working its change by construction, before any one has perceived that that invisible and helpless worm has been busily employed in consuming its substance. In truth, man is not made to be trusted for life, if secured against all liability to account.[9]

Can anyone in all honesty deny the assessment of Jefferson's statement? He referred to the Supreme Court's decisions as an "invisible and helpless worm" that is busy "consuming its substance" before anyone realizes what has happened. According to Jefferson, the Supreme Court's oligarchic power resulted from the lifetime appointment of the justices, which led to lack of accountability. Jefferson is saying that no one should be free from accountability—not any individual and not any branch of government.

Dr. Thomas Abshier agrees with Jefferson's assessment when he says, "We have allowed the Supreme Court rulings to exert the legal effect of a Constitutional Amendment over our legal and social system. But, such Power over the group moral state was not intended by the Founders."[10]

This usurpation of power by the Supreme Court has been referred to as "judicial legislation." The Supreme Court has elevated their own status above the legislature, the executive office, and above the people. Some think of them as a ruling totalitarian government, which is a dictatorship by committee. I think the more accurate description is that the Supreme Court is now a committee of kings.

Some commentators think that judicial legislation is necessary. William Bondy defends judicial legislation, claiming that "the English system of judicial interpretation in some cases must inevitably result in judicial legislation."[11] This, he claims, is because imperfectly written laws in which the intent is impossible to determine "by rules of construction" require interpretation, which is supplied by the Courts. In such instances, "the judge is called upon to determine what the law should be. The judge thus becomes a legislator."[12] In these instances, though, the judge ought not add anything beyond the intent of the law.

What is more worrisome, though, are these words, also by Bondy: "It is an indisputable fact that, notwithstanding the separation of powers, the principles and distinctions established by the decision of single cases become a part of the law of the land. Until overridden by express statutes, judicial precedents become a system of rules binding all."[13] In other words, judges legislate from the bench, binding all citizens—and the executive and legislative branches of our government—to the decisions of the few.

Abshier argued that there must be true balance among the branches of government:

> The Legislature must consider the issue of Constitutionality in every new law it passes. The Supreme Court has every right to judge an act of Congress as Constitutional, but the Legislature has a right to override a Supreme Court judgment they deemed unconstitutional. Ultimately, any new principle of government that fundamentally alters the original intent and spirit of the Constitution must be referred to the people for Amendment. Likewise, the Executive branch should protest and refuse to execute a Supreme Court judgment deemed unlawful and unconstitutional. Such Executive action against the Supreme Court is the equivalent of a Presidential veto of Congressional acts.
>
> Thus, each branch has an essentially equal obligation to judge the Constitutionality of the acts, laws, and judgments of the other branches. Unless the system contains the mechanisms by which one branch may overrule the other, we risk the concentration of power that the founders sought to embed in our system of Separation of powers. To vest sole authority to judge Constitutionality in the Judiciary puts us at risk of falling prey to the whims and enforced ideology of these 9 Black Robed Oligarchs."[14]

This opinion seems to reflect the thoughts of Andrew Jackson in a message to veto the banks of the United States:

> It is as much the duty of the House of Representatives, of the Senate, and of the President to decide upon the constitutionality of any bill or resolution which may be presented to them for passage or approval as it is the supreme judges when it may be brought before them for judicial decision. The opinion of the judges has no more authority over Congress than the opinion of Congress has over the judges, and on that point the President is independent of both. The authority of the Supreme Court must not, therefore, be permitted to control the Congress or the Executive when acting in their legislative capacities, but to have only such influence as the force of their reasoning may deserve."[15]

Read that again: "The authority of the Supreme Court *must not... be permitted* to control the Congress or the Executive when acting in their legislative capacities" (emphasis added). Why has it become accepted that the judicial branch controls the Constitution? Why has it become normative that the executive and legislative branches are subject to the legislative agenda of the Supreme Court?

Abraham Lincoln, in his first inaugural address, said, "If the policy of the government... is to be irrevocably fixed by decision of the Supreme Court... the people will have ceased, to be their own rulers, having, to that extent, practically resigned their government, into the hands of that eminent tribunal."[16] Addressing the legal challenges facing the nation regarding slavery and secession from the union, he continued, "Unanimity is impossible; the rule of a minority, as a permanent arrangement, is wholly inadmissible; so that, rejecting the majority principle, anarchy, or despotism in some form, is all that is left."[17]

According to Lincoln, recognized as one of our greatest presidents, we the people will have lost our government when American policy is established by the Supreme Court. Not only this, but he warns against the opinion of the few outweighing the opinion of the majority. Nonetheless, many contemporary Supreme Court decisions are what are called "5-4 decisions," which means that they are approved by five out of nine justices. Rather than being made by elected members of Congress or the president, many pivotal changes are established by a handful of president-appointed and Senate-approved Supreme Court justices. The Supreme Court, the highest body of the judicial branch of government, does not answer to the people, which should be the final authority. This disregard for the majority opinion, much less the opinion of our forefathers, is yet another representation of America's move toward secular humanism.

This anti-Christian, anti-religious religion contradicts the foundation of American government. John Quincy Adams said, "The highest glory of the American Revolution was this; it connected in one indissoluble bond the principles of civil government with the principles of Christianity."[18]

Justice Antonin Scalia scolded the Court with these words: "The Court must be living in another world. Day by day, case by case, it is busy designing a Constitution for a country I do not recognize."[19] Unfortunately for us, the executive and legislative branches have acquiesced to the Supreme Court, have stood by, and have watched from the sidelines as the Supreme Court continues to destroy the underpinnings of this nation. While elected officials fail to act, the Courts continue to establish secular humanism as America's religion. The Christian Broadcasting Network's Pat Robertson issues this warning:

> The Supreme Court is the last bastion of liberal power. For over forty years, black-robed tyrants have pushed a radical agenda in America with devastating results. Consider the damage inflicted since 1962:
>
> They banished prayer and the Bible from our public schools.
>
> They raised a "right of privacy" banner, under which 43 million babies have been aborted.
>
> They overthrew sodomy laws, opening the door to same-sex marriage.
>
> They called for the removal of the Ten Commandments from Courthouses across the nation.[20]

There are many frightening examples of the abuse of power by the courts. In his book *Persecution*, David Limbaugh gives an account of how far some judges will go to trample free speech in a ruling by a judge toward a high school graduation ceremony.

> In May 1995, Samuel B. Kent, U.S. District judge for the Southern District of Texas, decreed that any student uttering the word "Jesus" would be arrested and incarcerated for six months. Lest you think this was some month-late April Fools' joke,

> the judge expressly avowed his earnestness in his official order. His ruling stated, in part:
>
> "And make no mistake, the Court is going to have a United States marshal in attendance at the graduation. If any student offends this Court, that student will be summarily arrested and will face up to six months incarceration in the Galveston County Jail for contempt of Court. Anyone who thinks I'm kidding about this order better think again.... Anyone who violates these orders, no kidding, is going to wish that he or she had died as a child when this Court gets through with it."[21]

Is Judge Kent serious when he arrogantly and abusively threatens teenagers with such punishment for mentioning the name of Jesus at their graduation? If he believes that anyone who would dare pray in the name of Jesus on public property should be made to wish they were never born, the history of our country would be far different. Here are a few of the names Judge Kent would seek to deny freedom: George Washington, John Adams, Thomas Jefferson, Patrick Henry, Benjamin Franklin, John Quincy Adams, Abraham Lincoln, James Madison, Theodore Roosevelt, Andrew Jackson, and Ronald Reagan. America is very fortunate that Judge Kent never had these patriots in his court.

Another headline in recent years read "Judge: Legislative Prayers Can't Mention Jesus." According to the article, "Prayers that typically open sessions of the Indiana House of Representatives can no longer mention Jesus Christ or advance a religious denomination, a federal judge ruled Wednesday." U.S. District Court Judge David Hamilton issued the ruling that "the practice of the Indiana House shown by the evidence here amounts in practical terms to an official endorsement of the Christian religion."[22] Judge Hamilton ordered, "Plaintiffs are entitled to a permanent injunction against the Speaker in his official capacity barring him from permitting sectarian prayer as part of the official proceedings of the Indiana House of Representatives. If the Speaker chooses to continue any form of legislative prayer, he shall advise persons offering such a prayer (a) that it must be nonsectarian and must not be used to proselytize or advance any one faith or belief or to disparage any other faith or belief, and (b) that they should refrain from using Christ's name or title or any other denominational appeal."[23] Indiana House of Representatives Speaker Brian Bosma responded to Hamilton's ruling by calling it "the first step to completely remove the opportunity to express ourselves in accordance with our faith.... It's absolutely wrong. It's absolutely intolerable."[24]

For nearly 190 years, the Indiana House included prayer, yet one man overruled the decision. A single judge abused his position and dictated against the long-standing practice and will of the legislative body of the state of Indiana.[25] Again, the few seeks to outweigh the many; the one seeks to displace the majority.

In 2005, a U.S. District Judge ruled against "intelligent design." The story reported by The Associated Press said, "U.S. District Judge John E. Jones delivered a stinging attack on the Dover Area School Board, saying its first-in-the-nation decision in October, 2004, to insert intelligent design into the science curriculum violates the constitutional separation of church and state."[26] The secular humanist agenda demands that scientific theories that include the possibility of a God are by definition religion and not science. But is not science "systematic knowledge of the physical or material world gained through observation and experimentation"?[27] Are not Christians permitted to observe and experiment, then conclude that there is a divine cause for all that is? And are not scientific theories—I speak of theories here, not of facts, which exist as well—simply that: theories? Another definition of *science* is "a branch of knowledge or study dealing with a body of facts or truths systematically arranged and showing the operation of general laws."[28] Are theories by this definition excluded from science? Of course not! But theories are not provable—at least, have not yet been proven—and therefore should be acknowledged as theories.

Consider the words of British professor and former atheist Antony Flew: "What I think the DNA material has done is show that intelligence must have been involved in getting these extraordinarily diverse elements together. The enormous complexity by which the results were achieved look to me like the work of intelligence."[29] According to Cliff Kincaid, author of the article in which this quote appeared, "Flew told AP [Associated Press] that his current ideas had some similarity with those of U.S. 'intelligent design' theorists, who believe the complexity of life points to an intelligent source of life, rather than the random and natural processes posited by Charles Darwin's theory of evolution."[30] Kincaid calls Flew "the world's best-known atheist" and writes that Flew "has cited advancements in science as proof of the existence of God."[31]

Professor Flew also gave an interview to Dr. Gary R. Habermas, professor of philosophy and theology at Liberty University, where he discussed his journey from atheism to theism. He said, "Darwin himself, in the fourteenth chapter of *The Origin of Species*, pointed out that his whole argument began with a being which already possessed reproductive powers. This is the creature the evolution of which a truly comprehensive theory of evolution must give some account. Darwin himself was well aware that he had not produced such an account. It now seems to me that the findings of more than fifty years of DNA research have provided materials for a new and enormously powerful argument for design."[32]

Flew also addressed the subject of teaching morality in secular schools. He continued, "The Supreme Court has utterly misinterpreted the clause in the Constitution about not establishing a religion: misunderstanding it as imposing a ban on all official reference to religion."[33] If scientific experimentation and observation lead one to posit the existence of God, why is it impermissible to teach that possibility in the classroom?

Having said this, I agree with Judge Jones that intelligent design, or creationism, is not a scientific fact that can be proved by scientific methods. However, I also believe that evolution and certain other scientific assertions are theories and, therefore, are taken on faith. Since the judges ruled that intelligent design cannot be taught because it is a theory, then why is evolution taught? In this, Christians and secular humanists share the same ground; the difference is that we admit to our faith, rather than deceive ourselves into believing that we are above or beyond it. Hebrews 11:6 says, "But without faith it is impossible to please Him, for he who comes to God must believe that He is, and that He is a rewarder of those who diligently seek Him." God will not submit to man's test; rather, man must submit to His test. Therefore, you cannot please God without faith. Though we may not be able to empirically prove the reality of intelligent design, we may be personally acquainted with the Creator, the intellect behind it.

Finally, I strongly disagree with Judge Jones's statement that teaching intelligent design "violates the Constitutional separation of church and state." Neither Judge Jones nor anyone else can show where the Constitution mentions the word *separation* regarding church and state. This is merely a catchword the courts use to justify their decisions regarding any case before them that pertains to religion.

If Judge Jones insists that he evolved from a lower form of life, that is his privilege, but I will reject any such nonsense regarding my own life. I believe the Bible when it says I am made in the image of God (Gen. 1:26). Judge Jones might look at me and come to the conclusion that I was not made in the image of God, but when I look at him, I will still believe He was created by an intelligent Being.

Judges may outlaw religion in school, but the writings and actions of the framers of the Constitution and leaders throughout the centuries have believed in and affirmed a divine Creator. Judges refer to a wall of separation between government and religion, a concept foreign to the Constitution. Chief Justice William Rehnquist wrote in *Wallace v. Jaffree*, "There is simply no historical foundation for the proposition that the framers intended to build a wall of separation [between the Church and State]....The recent Court decisions are in no way based on either the language or intent of the framers."[34] Yet, I would be willing to accept such a wall if the courts would stay on their side of it! The problem is that while the courts continue to make decisions based upon a phantom or invisible wall, they have no compunction or reluctance whatsoever to impose themselves on the religious side of the wall.

This is what the framers of our Constitution feared. Many Americans left England because the head that wore the crown and the head of the church were one and the same. Now, we have a very similar situation. The judiciary branch is now head of the government because it has usurped the power to overrule the other branches and judge what is and is not constitutional. It has seized the headship of the church in that it now limits the freedom of Christians to worship when and where they choose. And, perhaps most egregious of all, it has established secular humanism as the only religion permitted in schools and on government property. Therefore, the Supreme Court is now, along with their judiciary function, a judicial legislature and a judicial executive branch.

Why do the courts not recognize they have scaled the wall and crossed over into realms foreign to their design and purpose? They demand that religion stay on one side of the wall, away from government, but then they continue to interfere and control religion's side of the wall. They are a study in dangerous contradictions.

I refer the reader again to the words of Theodore Roosevelt: "It is the people, not the judges, who are entitled to say what their constitution means, for the constitution is theirs, it belongs to them and not to their servants in office—any other theory is incompatible with the foundation principles of our government"[35] The wise forefathers of this country established and supported a type of society where Christian faith, worship, and practice were encouraged, and followed it for nearly two hundred years. Now, activist judges claim to know more about what the Constitution means than the people who wrote it.

The question that remains is, why has Congress allowed

activist judges to become the masters instead of the servants of the people of this country? The control usurped by the judges is as dangerous as a power-hungry dictator. The members of Congress have been too busy playing party politics to understand they have become largely figureheads. They address their business responsibilities, but the judiciary branch makes the important decisions.

Failed Justice

Yet, these judges who are harsh towards Christians and religious speech are often lenient toward true criminals. The tenor of the court to protect militant dissidents and people of non-traditional sexual orientation is demonstrated by a decision of Judge Edward Cashman in Vermont. WCAX-TV's Brian Joyce reported this story in Burlington, Vermont, on January 4, 2005; the headline on the Web version reads, "Rapist's Prison Sentence Triggers Outrage." The outrage was aimed at Judge Cashman, who sentenced a man to a mere sixty days in jail after he was convicted of raping a little girl many times over a four-year span. Although prosecutors had recommended a minimum of an eight-year sentence, the judge disagreed, saying he didn't believe punishment works. Fortunately, community outrage influenced Judge Cashman to change his sentence to a minimum of three years in prison before the convicted man would be eligible for parole.[36]

Fox News Channel talk show host Bill O'Reilly, host of the television program *The O'Reilly Factor*, is an outspoken critic of soft sentencing for offenders. He took on an Ohio county court judge in 2006 after the judge sentenced a man who admitted to sexually abusing two young boys to probation alone. Franklin County Court Judge John Conner was lenient to the man who abused the two boys over a three-year period, even though the man had already been indicted two years before on twenty counts of rape and two counts of gross sexual imposition.[37]

O'Reilly also covered the story of the tragic rape and murder of Jessica Marie Lunsford, a nine year old girl who was killed by a sexual predator with previous convictions. This brutal murder sparked an outrage, with concerned parents and lawmakers in many states proposing bills to enact Jessica's Law. The original law, first enacted in Florida, mandates a minimum sentence of twenty-five years for first-time sexual offenders whose victims are under the age of twelve.[38]

On his Web site, O'Reilly reveals the following examples of failed justice:

- In Rhode Island, an eighteen year old teen was convicted of having sex with a thirteen year old girl, but received a sentence of probation. A couple of years later, he molested a fourteen year old girl, but served only one year. Later, he raped a sixteen year old girl and served only three years.

- In Missouri, a nineteen year old man admitted to sexually abusing a little girl beginning when she was only eight years old. His sentence? Four months prison; five years probation.

- In Minnesota, a man who had served sixteen years for raping a boy at gunpoint was released on $15,000 bail after he was accused of molesting another young boy. He then skipped

> bail and left for Idaho, where he is accused of kidnapping, raping, and killing a nine year old boy, as well as molesting [the little boy's] sister and killing the children's family.[39]

It would be quite a debate to determine whether these judges are guilty of malfeasance in office or of treason. These examples and headlines demonstrate that the judges have lost their values—what is good and what is evil, and what is right and what is wrong. By ignoring the history of this country, establishing secular humanism as the law of the land, and taking a soft stance against criminals, the courts often contradict the criteria they supposedly use in rendering their decisions. In so doing, they have placed America at risk.

Which Precedent?

Precedent is a criterion cited many times in making court judgments. I submit the following Supreme Court decision that should be viewed as precedent.

In *Church of the Holy Trinity v. United States* (1892), the Supreme Court said, "Our laws and our institutions must necessarily be based upon and embody the teachings of the Redeemer of mankind. It is impossible that it should be otherwise; and in this sense and to this extent our civilization and our institutions are emphatically Christian."[40]

What also should be considered is intent. Does the Supreme Court interpret the Constitution in light of its own agenda—that is, as a living document, malleable per the whims of the day and conformable to the doctrine of secular humanism—or in light of the intent of the framers of the Constitution? Justice William J. Brennan has made clear the answer. In explaining his opinion that prayer in public schools is unconstitutional, he wrote:

> Whatever Jefferson or Madison would have thought of Bible reading or the recital of the Lord's Prayer in... public schools,... our use of the history... must limit itself to broad purposes, not specific practices.... [The] Baltimore and Abington schools offend the First Amendment because they sufficiently threaten in our day those substantive evils the fear of which called forth the Establishment Clause....[Our] interpretation of the First Amendment must necessarily be responsive to the much more highly charged nature of religious questions in contemporary society. A too literal quest for the advice of the Founding Fathers upon the issues of these cases seems to me futile and misdirected.[41]

This means that the quotes marshaled in this book from the founding fathers and the presidents of the United States would hardly sway Justice Brennan. He seeks not their advice, their opinion, or their intent in framing that which he is charged with upholding. Their roles in our country's formation and history have become irrelevant.

So here we have a fundamental disagreement between secular humanist enablers and traditional Christians. Whereas original intent is irrelevant to the former, it is critical to us. Whereas the wisdom of those who have forged the path and framed the structure before us is not required by humanists, it is necessary for us. Whereas they perceive the bedrock of American civilization to be mere puffery, it is the foundation upon which we stake our lives for the good of all humankind.

Quoted earlier, Madison said, "We have staked the whole future of our new nation not upon the power of government; far from it. We have staked the future of all our political constitutions upon the capacity of each of ourselves to govern ourselves according to the moral principles of the Ten Commandments."[42]

In his May 16, 1982, National Day of Prayer Proclamation, Ronald Reagan eloquently reminded us of a time when dependence on God was the norm: "It's been written that the most sublime picture in American history was George Washington on his knees in the snow at Valley Forge. He personified a people who knew that it is not enough to depend on their own courage and goodness, that they must seek help from God—our Father and Preserver."[43]

Harvard University, chartered in 1636, instructed its first students:

> Let every Student be plainly instructed, and earnestly pressed to consider well, the maine end of his life and studies is, *to know God and Jesus Christ which is eternal life*, Joh. 17.3. and therefore to lay *Christ* in the bottome, as the only foundation of all sound knowledge and Learning. And seeing the Lord only giveth wisedome, Let every one seriously set himselfe by prayer in secret to seeke it of him, *Prov. 2.3.*"[44]

That which began in prayer, in an earnest desire to worship God freely, has been changed by those who wish to control and coerce. Woodrow Wilson issued this warning: "The government which was designed for the people has got into the hands of the bosses and their employers, the special interests. An invisible empire has been set up above the forms of democracy."[45] This invisible empire embodies the principles and values of secular humanism. The U.S. judiciary has promoted this ideology. By rejecting the intent of the framers of the Constitution, they have disrespected and dishonored the Constitution they swore to uphold.

What can be done? An important action is to reestablish balance between the three branches of government; the courts have disproportionate power only if the other branches cede it to them. The Constitutional Restoration Act to restore religious freedom and to restrict judicial jurisdiction was introduced in both the House and the Senate in 2004 and 2005. The bill includes the following language: "Notwithstanding any other provision of this chapter, the Supreme Court shall not have jurisdiction to review...any matter to the extent that relief is sought against an entity of Federal, State, or local government, or against an officer or agent of Federal, State, or local government (whether or not acting in official or personal capacity), concerning that entity's, officer's, or agent's acknowledgment of God as the sovereign source of law, liberty, or government."[46] Concerning jurisdiction, the bill continues:

> To the extent that a justice of the Supreme Court of the United States or any judge of any Federal Court engages in any activity that exceeds the jurisdiction of the Court of that justice or judge, as the case may be, by reason of section 1260 or 1370 of title 28, United States Code, as added by

> this Act, engaging in that activity shall be deemed to constitute the commission of—
>
> (1) an offense for which the judge may be removed upon impeachment and conviction; and
>
> (2) a breach of the standard of good behavior required by article III, section 1 of the Constitution.[47]

As of this writing, each bill has been referred to Senate and House sub-committees, respectively.

Quoted earlier, Thomas Jefferson warned of vesting power in the few. Patrick Henry echoes this concern, saying, "The Constitution is not an instrument for government to restrain the people, it is an instrument for the people to restrain the government—lest it come to dominate our lives and interests."[48] Ronald Reagan agreed, stating that "concentrated power has always been the enemy of liberty."[49] Historian Lord John Acton said, "Power tends to corrupt, and absolute power corrupts absolutely."[50]

If we do not curb the power of the Supreme Court and the lower courts, we will have no freedom, no control, and, ultimately, no nation we recognize or want to claim as our own.

Chapter 7
ANTI-CHRISTIAN MILITANT GROUPS

MANY FORCES ARE AT WORK IN AMERICA supporting the secular humanist agenda or other anti-Christian agendas. The common thread for these groups, even when they oppose each other, is their threat to the liberties that have made America great. We can get a handle on these attacks through examining the American Civil Liberties Union (ACLU) and atheism, both representing a continuation of the secular humanist attack, and Islamofascism.

The ACLU

The ACLU takes positions against the public utilization of many religious and, specifically, Christian expressions. It is the most active and successful organization in removing historic freedoms from the American people. The ACLU opposes prayers, religious ceremonies, and moments of silence in public schools; opposes government-sponsored displays of religious symbols on public property; supports abortion; supports civil rights for homosexual couples; and supports decriminalization of illegal drugs.

The ACLU rejects the accusation of a bias against Christians, claiming, "The ACLU vigorously defends the right of Americans to practice religion. But because the ACLU is often better known for its work preventing the government from promoting and funding selected religious activities, it is often wrongly assumed that the ACLU does not zealously defend the rights of religious believers, including Christians, to practice their religion." Cases "where the ACLU even defended the rights of religious believers to condemn homosexuality or abortion . . . reveal just how mistaken such assumptions are."[1] While it is true that in certain instances the ACLU has defended Christian rights, it is also true that the preponderance of cases the ACLU presses violate the principles of traditional Christians. Further, whatever the intent of individual ACLU leaders or lawyers, the ACLU misunderstands the intent of the founders and the founding documents, misunderstands the First Amendment's Establishment Clause, and uses the courts to suppress religious freedoms.

Commenting on a restraining order against prayer during graduation exercises at Russell County High School in Kentucky, an ACLU attorney said, "Our founders intended that these religious decisions be made by individuals and families, not the government."[2] We have already addressed in this book the issue of the founders' intent, which causes one to wonder which founders this attorney has read. It certainly was not Jefferson, Washington, Adams, Henry, or any other I have found. When the courts distort the First Amendment—as they have—and read into it what is not there—as they have—it is not surprising that contemporary lawyers, judges, and even citizens fail to recognize the history of their nation and the truth and intent of its founding documents. When citizens and lawmakers worship at the altar of secular humanism, it is not surprising that they spout the dogma of their religion.

On the ACLU Web site are many press releases regarding legal action prohibiting prayer in school: "Supreme Court Lets Ban on Coerced Prayer at Virginia Military Institute

Stand;"[3] "West VA School District Ends Graduation Prayer Policy; Student's Lawsuit 'Educated' Officials;"[4] "In Long-Awaited Victory, High Court Vacates Alabama Decision Allowing Public School Prayer;"[5] "ACLU Asks Virginia School Boards Not to Open Meetings with Prayer;"[6] and "In Victory for Religious Liberty, Unanimous Appeals Court Finds LA's School Prayer Law Unconstitutional."[7]

Religious symbols are also under attack by the ACLU. In Missouri, the organization led a fight to remove the fish symbol from the logo of the city of Republic. In ruling in favor of the ACLU, Judge Russell G. Clark said; "When viewing the fish on Republic's flag, a reasonable observer would conclude that it is a Christian religious symbol. While the citizens of Republic may have intended that its seal send only a message of moral values or promote 'a universal symbol of religion,' an applaudable motive cannot save the city seal from a violation of the Establishment Clause. While the purpose of placing the fish on the city seal may not have been to endorse Christianity, the effect of the seal is to do so."[8]

While defending itself against the charge of leading a war on Christmas, the ACLU writes, "Christmas displays, for example—things like nativity displays—are perfectly acceptable at homes and churches. Religious expression—during the holidays and throughout the year—is a valued part of the First Amendment rights guaranteed all citizens. But government should never be in the business of endorsing things like religious displays."[9] This argument fails to understand that the free expression of religion in public, in courthouses, in legislatures, in schools, or anywhere else is not the establishment of religion. Rather, *free expression* is the strongest bulwark *against* the establishment of religion. The second problem, as noted in previous chapters, is that it is impossible to banish religion without establishing religion; that is, the prohibition of religion is the establishment of anti-religion.

Regarding abortion, the ACLU has what it calls the Reproductive Freedom Project. Its director says, "The ability to control when and whether to have children is absolutely essential for women to be able to participate equally in society.... So much of the ACLU's work—from racial justice to lesbian and gay rights to women's and immigrants' rights—is tied together by a belief that everyone has the right to make personal decisions about their intimate relationships free from government interference."[10] It is hypocritical that the ACLU invokes a "free from government interference" claim when it consistently uses the courts to interfere with the rights of the religious to express themselves.

The ACLU opposes "value-laden speech" by a doctor prior to an abortion. Commenting on a lawsuit filed by Planned Parenthood against a South Dakota law requiring doctors to counsel women prior to abortion "that the abortion ends 'the life of a whole, separate, unique, living human being' with whom she has a preexisting relationship protected under the law," the ACLU contends that "such requirements would gravely interfere in medical practice and women's personal decision making."[11] As the ACLU defines it, *personal decision-making* means that the abortion industry should not be required to help a woman make a more informed choice by sharing with her moral value in support of the unborn, the single most vulnerable constituency in the world. It is blatantly contradictory that the ACLU proclaims the act of performing an abortion to be value-neutral, while actions like flag burning are passionately defended as valuable "free speech."[12] It is noteworthy that the ACLU claims that abortion providers are engaged in the practice of "abortion care."[13]

The ACLU considers same-sex marriage a civil rights issue. In applauding a decision by the Vermont Supreme Court to give same-sex couples the same "common benefits and protections" as married couples, an ACLU press release said, "The American Civil Liberties Union, which filed a friend-of-the-Court brief in the case, hailed the ruling—the nation's first—as a pivotal moment for civil rights in the '90s." Matthew Coles, director of the ACLU's Lesbian and Gay Rights Project, said, "Never mind the millennium, for gay and lesbian couples, a new era began today." He called this decision "full equality, and that is an historic first."[14]

In 2006, the ACLU filed a lawsuit against the State of Maryland, "charging that it is a violation of state constitution to deny same-sex couples the ability to marry and the many family protections that come with marriage." After Baltimore City Circuit Court Judge Brooke Murdock agreed, ACLU attorney Ken Choe commented, "The Court was right to conclude that preventing same-sex couples from marrying is sex discrimination." According to the press release, the judge "found that there is not even a rational basis for denying same-sex couples the ability to marry."[15]

The point is not that the ACLU is forcing heterosexual couples to become homosexual. The point is that they are forcing cultural definitions that are based on the dominant morality to be changed to accommodate homosexual lifestyles. A society has the right to define its institutions as it sees fit, as long as it doesn't impinge on the rights of those who disagree.

In November 2003, the ACLU articulated talking points to frame the same-sex marriage debate. These suggestions included: "Frame the debate as 'denying the right to marry' and 'discrimination.' Avoid talking about 'recognizing,' 'allowing' or 'supporting' gay marriage. Without attacking the tradition of marriage directly, remind people that there comes a time when our country breaks with traditions that wrongly . . . discriminate against individuals."[16]

The ACLU and its affiliates receive funding from well-known foundations. According to a 2004 *New York Times* article, the ACLU rejected money from the Ford and Rockefeller foundations, both of which require the organizations they support to sign a grant agreement promising that the organization will not engage in or promote terrorist activity. Why? Because the foundations' "effort to ensure that none of their money inadvertently underwrites terrorism or other unacceptable activities is a threat to civil liberties."[17]

Secular humanism has effectively paired the ACLU with activist judges, a marriage made somewhere other than in heaven. The ACLU brings the case; the courts legislate the law.

Is it curious that the minority must not be offended, but the majority may be offended at every turn? Hans Zeiger reports on the ACLU attack against the Pledge of Allegiance:

> The Pledge of Allegiance is doing irreparable harm to the minds and hearts of America's school children. So alleges an ACLU lawsuit against the state of Colorado for its new law requiring the daily recitation of the Pledge of Allegiance in public schools.

> This time, it isn't just about "One Nation Under God." Now, the American Civil Liberties Union wants to get rid of the whole pledge. On August 12, the ACLU filed suit in federal district Court on behalf of 'students and teachers throughout the state' who seem to be offended by the notion of the republic for which the flag stands, unity, liberty, and justice for all.[18]

Why is someone offended by the Pledge of Allegiance to the flag of the United States of America in America? They are not forced to make the pledge. Why should citizens not have the opportunity to express in public their support of an allegiance to their own country? The few people who are offended are pressing a legal attack through organizations such as the ACLU to keep the rest of the population from doing anything that might offend them. I confess: my entire life, my being and soul, and everything I stand for are probably an offence to them. Conversely, their actions regarding America and God are an offense to me, but I'm not suing them over it.

Author, actor, and television show host Ben Stein said, "I don't like getting pushed around for being a Jew and I don't think Christians like getting pushed around for being Christians. I think people who believe in God are sick and tired of getting pushed around, period. I have no idea where the concept came from that America is an explicitly atheist country. I can't find it in the Constitution and I don't like it being shoved down my throat."[19]

In the end, the ACLU is an advocacy group. It is telling that the organization has a strategy for putting a spin on hard questions. In the ACLU talking points document on same-sex marriage, two statements provide responses to questions regarding the impact of same-sex marriage on young people and children: "Being gay is not a matter of choice—it is something you are born with. People cannot be persuaded to be gay or straight. It is just part of who they are;" and, "Allowing two people who are in a loving and committed long-term relationship to have legal protections will have a positive impact on the children they adopt, care for, or other children in their communities."[20]

Of course, in many or most instances, rather than posing arguments within the court of public opinion, they pose them in the courts themselves. Why convince when you can coerce by the power of the government?

Atheism

I am sure that ACLU members are diverse in their religious beliefs. But atheists, of course, simply do not believe in the existence of God.

In a supplement to the July, 1988, issue of *American Atheist* magazine, atheists celebrated the Supreme Court's *Murray v. Curlett* decision by reprinting the Court's opinion. The case was filed by Madalyn Murray O'Hair in response to the Baltimore, Maryland, public schools' requirement that students participate in Bible reading and prayer. The introduction to the online version of the supplement said, "Just 25 years ago, June 17, 1963, the Supreme Court of the United States kicked reverential Bible reading and prayer recitation out of the nation's public schools."[21] This article aptly describes the action of the Supreme Court in this ruling as *kicking* Bible reading and prayer out of our public schools. It bothers me greatly that any atheist or other minority opinion can take legal action to stop patriotic or religious expressions by merely stating that it "offends" them.

Remember that secular humanists "deploy efforts... to seek to explain the world in supernatural terms, and to look outside nature for salvation."[22] They also consider education "a most powerful ally of Humanism, and every American public school is a school of Humanism."[23] Is it any wonder, then, that atheists attack the Bible and religious expression in the schools? Naturally, they want that forum exclusively for their agenda, their ideologies, and under their control.

Islamofascism

Atheists and the ACLU represent a secular humanist agenda in America; but there is another insidious force: Islamofascism. Instead of being atheistic, this force is fanatically theistic, but nonetheless anti-Christian.

Islam represents the second largest religion in the world at 1.5 billion adherents.[24] By some estimates, it is the fastest growing religion.[25] Given the militancy of many of its adherents, these facts should cause concern.

I am not prejudiced against any nationality or ethnicity. I love the German people and visit there when I can. Some of my best friends and some very wonderful people are Germans. While I am not prejudiced against Germans, I am prejudiced against the Nazism that once dominated Germany. I visited Russia when it was part of the Soviet bloc, visited Romania under the despotic rule of Nicolae Ceauşescu, and visited many other communist countries. Again, I have very good friends in some of these countries. I haven't any prejudice against the people, but I am prejudiced against the communism that controlled many in these countries and still oppresses many people around the globe today.

I have Arab friends as well, and I am not prejudiced against Arabs. But I admit that I am prejudiced against any group or religion determined to force its will, religion, or dogma upon other people, even to the point of murder and terror.

Brigitte Gabriel was a victim of radical Islam. As a child in Lebanon, she and her family lived years underground, literally, in a bomb shelter, following a jihad against Lebanese Christians. She writes, "The United States has been a prime target of radical Islamic hatred and terror. Every Friday, mosques in the Middle East ring with shrill prayers and monotonous chants that call down death, destruction, and damnation on America and its people."[26]

Oliver North quotes Ms. Gabriel in a 2006 speech to the Intelligence Summit in Washington, DC, saying, "Tolerating evil is a crime. Appeasing murderers doesn't buy protection, it earns disrespect and loathing in the enemy's eyes. Apathy is the weapon by which the west is committing suicide. Political correctness is a shackle around our ankles by which Islamists are leading us to our demise."[27]

While many Muslims are not terrorists, in America and around the world many have joined the chorus of the offended. As mentioned earlier, the tone and body language of John Hagee on television offended some of them. According to a report in *The Scotsman*, Burger King ice cream cone lids offended a Muslim because "the design resembled the Arabic inscription for Allah." With the man threatening a jihad, the fast-food chain "is being forced to spend thousands of pounds redesigning the lid with backing from The Muslim Council of Britain."[28]

The list of offenses is long, indeed, including cartoons, books, history, operas, and more. But the strategy is working. According to James Joyner, "Oddly, the barbaric reaction to art and other forms of speech is having its desired chilling effect. We've had the network behind 'South Park,' which doesn't blink twice at showing...all manner of vile representations of Jesus Christ refusing to show a cartoon image of Muhammad."[29] The few have intimidated the many. Now the politically correct position is not to offend the offenders but, instead, to offend the victims.

In early 2008, a *Times of London* article reported that "a children's story based on the tale of the Three Little Pigs was rejected for an award after judges became concerned that it would offend Muslims." The company that produced the CD-ROM claimed that Muslims, among others, had voiced support; but the judges refused to recommend the virtual book aimed at children.[30]

Islamists are very active in the Western world, attacking Christianity and many public expressions of Christianity. Radical Islamists and other more conservative Muslims enjoy the freedom of religion and freedom of speech in America, but many use these same freedoms to deny Americans their rights.

While Muslims claim to be offended by Christianity in America, Christians are murdered in Muslim countries. In Turkey, Muslim Turks killed three Christians, cutting their throats. What prompted their murder? "They are attacking our religion," claimed notes in the murderers' pockets.[31] In Nigeria, Islamists murdered 130 Christians because they were offended by cartoons depicting Muhammad that were published in Denmark.[32] In Ethiopia, a mob of three hundred Islamists killed six Christians—including two priests and two elderly women—and injured fifteen others. The Christians were in a midnight worship service when the mob poured fire around the church, forcing the worshipers out of the building, then attacked them.[33] If Muslims may protest against Burger King cups and cartoons, why are Christians not willing to vocally protest the murder of innocent believers at the hands of radicals?

In Afghanistan, converting to Christianity is a crime against Islam, punishable by death. In 2006, Abdul Rahman, an Afghan who had been a practicing Christian for sixteen years, was detained for prosecution due to his Christianity. The judge overseeing the trial said he could escape punishment only if he were ruled insane. Rahman was released following international pressure and was given asylum in Italy.[34] This episode gives the Western world a disturbing glimpse into the reality of Islam.

Perhaps what is most disturbing of all is the silence of the Islamic community in the United States and elsewhere. It is not surprising when radicals and fanatics act in radical and fanatical ways. Many Muslims beg non-Muslims not to judge them by the actions of the Islamofascists, yet when the atrocities occur, where are their voices?

In "Selective Muslim Silence," Judith Apter Klinghoffer asks, "Where is the sane moderate peace loving Muslim world? Why is its voice so rarely raised in condemnation of Islamist atrocities?" She answers that, instead of vociferously condemning extremist acts, Muslim organizations "can be plenty vocal and aggressive when it comes to protecting

Islamists from the consequences of their own actions." After discussing the Danish cartoon issues, she concludes:

> So, here we are: part of the Muslim community is in the thrall of a totalitarian ideology which turns young Muslims into human bombs. Photos of Muslim and non Muslim civilian body parts flying in the middle of markets, mosques, discos and hotels have become routine. Beheadings of Christian and Jewish men and women are no longer surprising. And what do the ever-silent and passive-defensive Muslim countries, Organization of Islamic Conference and the Arab League vociferously condemn? They are condemning the publication of cartoons featuring Muhammad in a Danish paper. The absurdity of this action is only matched by its hypocrisy.[35]

Just as we should encourage the Christian community to speak out against misrepresentations of our faith by the actions of a few radical Christian believers, Muslims should be expected to likewise condemn with all their heart and soul the violence, intolerance, hatred, and terrorism of their Islamofascist brothers and sisters.

Chapter 8
FEDERAL GOVERNMENT ENCROACHMENT

Freedom is indivisible, there is no s on the end of it. You can erode freedom, diminish it, but you cannot divide it and choose to keep 'some freedoms' while giving up others.[1]

—Ronald Reagan

THE FRAMERS OF THE CONSTITUTION WERE CAREFUL to write a Constitution that would protect the citizens from an oppressive government. It is astounding to observe the changes in the federal government and to see how people have been robbed of their freedoms and abused the power of the government. There are many areas in which the government encroaches on the rights of American citizens.

The IRS

One means of encroachment is the Internal Revenue Department (IRS). Jay Sekulow explains the history of this intrusion in an article on the American Center for Law and Justice (ACLJ) Web site. Sekulow is chief counsel of the ACLJ, an organization based in Washington, DC, that specializes in constitutional law. I doubt any person or any organization in America is more effective in protecting the rights of citizens and churches than Mr. Sekulow and the ACLJ. I was privileged to hear Mr. Sekulow and some ACLJ staff advisers discuss some of these issues. Sekulow highlights America's history in including religious organizations in its political debate:

> The country has a rich and welcomed history of turning to churches and houses of worship during the debate of the great moral issues of the day. In the early days, the 'election sermon' was common—pastors acknowledging our religious heritage and addressing the key issues of their day.... During the revolutionary era, pastors spoke out from the pulpit encouraging dissent and calling for freedom—the prelude to the birth of our country—a country that cherishes free speech.[2]

He explains that the original purpose of the IRS, "to collect revenue for the general treasury," has changed to that of acting as "'speech police'—holding a heavy hand over non-profit organizations—including churches—threatening to remove their tax-exempt status if they participate in political activity." Sekulow traces this transformation to Lyndon B. Johnson who, as U.S. Senator, pushed an amendment disallowing tax-exempt organizations from engaging in politics with the penalty of losing their tax-exempt status. The result of this amendment passing into law has been, in Seculow's words, "flawed, misplaced, and a disaster." He writes, "The special power given to the IRS not only stifles the First Amendment rights of pastors and churches, but the IRS has been selective and biased in its enforcement."[3]

Sekulow concludes that this threat has the opposite consequence of what is needed and what is constitutionally protected. "Religious leaders not only have a constitutional right to address the moral issues of the day—many believe they have a responsibility to do so—especially in the context of political campaigns.... Under current IRS regulations, pastors and churches cannot endorse or oppose a candidate for political office. But they can—and should—speak out from the pulpit on issues that matter most, that are being debated this political season—issues like abortion, same-sex marriage, and the war on terrorism."[4]

The encroachment of government upon the freedom of religion should be the concern of every Christian, but the encroachment of government upon freedom of speech and other cherished freedoms should be of concern to every American. Robert Bork commented on an action of the U.S. Supreme Court regarding the protection of homosexual sex: "The Court... continued to view the First Amendment as a protection of self-gratification rather than of the free articulation of ideas, and overturned two hundred years of history to hold that political patronage is unconstitutional."[5] When we take "the free articulation of ideas" for granted, we risk losing them for ourselves and future generations.

The Department of Homeland Security

The Department of Homeland Security was created as a response to the attack on September 11, 2001, and most conservative Christians, as patriots, applauded the move. We wanted better security on our borders to protect us from those that hate America. However, as Americans have done so many times in the past, we make decisions in trust and fail to read the fine print. What first appeared as an agency created to protect us has cost us some of our most precious and cherished freedoms. The Department of Homeland Security has unprecedented authority and power to override freedoms that normally would have taken decades of erosion to accomplish.

Even from the beginning, voices were raised in concern regarding the potential encroachment on civil liberties via the Department of Homeland Security. An analysis by The Brookings Institute complained that the plan to create the department focused on reorganizing the executive branch, not on the role Congress would or should play.

> Proper congressional oversight is a crucial element of the overall homeland security effort. Congress provides an important independent perspective on executive branch proposals. It can hold agencies accountable and reflect public concerns about priorities and trade-offs, both for resources and for sensitive issues such as the appropriate balance between security and civil liberties.[6]

The Rutherford Institute Web site says, "Our government is becoming more and more intrusive. With the passage of sweeping laws such as the USA Patriot Act many find themselves questioning whether we really are living under Orwell's Big Brother government."[7] Regarding the USA Patriot Act—which provides greater surveillance and investigative authority to government law enforcement agencies, ostensibly to combat terrorism in the U.S.—Rutherford Institute president said, "Certain provisions of the USA Patriot Act reflect a steady assault on fundamental rights and liberties that has served only to make us less free, and not more secure."[8]

The Real ID Act

The Real ID Act (Public Law 109-13, signed into law May 11, 2005) is another terrifying act of both the Congress and the Bush Administration that brings us to the brink of a police state by increasing the requirements and standards for identification. It signals a loss of privacy and an alarming increase in government control over individuals' lives. A headline that is closer to the truth than many realize is "Real ID Act Passed—The End of America." The accompanying article reads, "The Real ID Act blackmails state governments into turning their drivers' license into a draconian tool of the federal homeland security apparatus.... In May 2008, barring a miracle, America as we once knew it will be in ruins."[9]

Bruce Schneier, founder and CTO of a global Internet security company and a member of the Advisory Board of the Electronic Privacy Information Center (EPIC), has been very vocal about the overreach of the Real ID law. He wrote in his Crypto-Gram newsletter, "The wackiest thing is that none of this [Real ID] is required. In October 2004, the Intelligence Reform and Terrorism Prevention Act of 2004 was signed into law. That law included stronger security measures for driver's licenses, the security measures recommended by the 9/11 Commission Report. That's already done. It's already law."[10] Schneier continues, "Real ID goes way beyond that. It's a huge power-grab by the federal government over the states' systems for issuing driver's licenses.... Combine Real ID with Secure Flight and you have an unprecedented system for broad surveillance of the population. Is there anyone who would feel safer under this kind of police state?"[11]

Of the measures applied to ensure that identification cards not complying with Real ID standards will be clearly recognizable, Schneier writes, "In its own guidance document, the department has proposed [metaphorically] branding citizens not possessing a Real ID card in a manner that lets all who see their official state-issued identification know that they're 'different,' and perhaps potentially dangerous, according to standards established by the federal government. They would become stigmatized, branded, marked, ostracized, segregated."[12] A similar concern is raised by the Electronic Privacy Information Center (EPIC). Melissa Ngo, Director of the EPIC Identification and Surveillance Project, was quoted in an EPIC press release, saying, "REAL ID creates a United States where individuals are either 'approved' or 'suspect,' and that is a real danger to security and civil rights."[13]

The concern is that while we are vigilant watching our borders, the federal government continues its encroachment upon the rights and freedoms of the states and the individuals. There is also a concern that the Real ID will become a national identification card. That which begins as one thing can often take on other roles (as our discussion of the IRS, above, recognizes).

In January 2008, the Department of Homeland Security made its final recommendations for state-issued licenses and identification cards. Thankfully, the department did not recommend a computer chip embedded in each person's driver's license that would contain personal identification.[14] Although this controversial measure did not make the final cut, will there come a time when it will be required?

I understand that the government must be vigilant in protecting its citizens from terrorists. I also understand that this responsibility weighs heavily on many government officials. Frankly, in today's climate with enemies outside and inside our borders, it's a difficult task. Without the right tools, it will be an impossible task.

At the same time, freedom is the critical foundation upon which the country was built—freedom of speech, freedom of religion, the right to privacy, and more. The government is an instrument of the people; the people are not the slaves of the government. Whereas many patriotic Americans, myself included, support efforts to protect all citizens from outside interests, we must also protect ourselves from a government that lapses in its judgment or intent.

I quoted Ronald Reagan earlier in this book as saying, "Concentrated power has always been the enemy of liberty."[15] But way back in 1964, long before the Reagan Revolution, he delivered a speech with these words: "If we lose freedom here, there is no place to escape to. This is the last stand on Earth. And this idea that government is beholden to the people, that it has no other source of power except to sovereign people, is still the newest and most unique idea in all the long history of man's relation to man."[16]

The government, whether federal, state, or local, is beholden to the people. This is a tremendous charge to those officials, both elected and appointed, who hold a sacred trust. It also means that all citizens have a responsibility to support, direct, voice ideas, enter the debates, and, as necessary, resist abuses.

I remind the citizens of this country again of Eisenhower's words: "If you want total security, go to prison. There you're fed, clothed, given medical care and so on. The only thing lacking... is freedom."[17]

May we be wise in considering the power we the people give our government.

Chapter 9
ANTI-ISRAEL POLITICAL FORCES

I MENTIONED EARLIER THAT ISRAEL AND AMERICA ARE favored of God. While God's favor upon America started with the colonies four hundred years ago, the covenant God made with Abraham thousands of years ago has endured the passage of time, circumstances, politics, power, and changes in the economy. God told Abraham in Genesis 12:2–3:

> I will make you a great nation; I will bless you and make your name great; And you shall be a blessing. I will bless those who bless you, And I will curse him who curses you; And in you all the families of the earth shall be blessed.

Observe God's promises to Abraham. God promised to make from Abraham a great nation and make his name great. He would bless those that aided and blessed Israel. He would curse those that cursed or did harm to Israel. Abraham's descendants in the earthly line would inherit this promised plot of land. The land given to Abraham was to belong to Israel forever. God promised the coming of the Messiah through Abraham and his seed, Isaac. He promised, "In you all the families of the earth shall be blessed."

God favored Israel still further.

> And I will establish My covenant between Me and you and your descendants after you in their

> generations, for an everlasting covenant, to be God to you and your descendants after you. Also I give to you and your descendants after you the land in which you are a stranger, all the land of Canaan, as an everlasting possession; and I will be their God.
>
> —Genesis 17:7–8

Canaan is a land grant given to Israel by God Himself. God gave Israel a deed title to the land and recorded the title in heaven. God established the boundaries of the territory and stated that it would belong to Israel forever: it was an everlasting possession established on an everlasting covenant that would exist as long as heaven and Earth existed.

The prophet Jeremiah details many of God's promises to Israel and then concludes with the promise that these promises are as certain as the ordinances of the universe, which will stand forever.

> Thus says the Lord, Who gives the sun for a light by day, The ordinances of the moon and the stars for a light by night, Who disturbs the sea, And its waves roar (The Lord of hosts is His name): "If those ordinances depart From before Me, says the Lord, Then the seed of Israel shall also cease From being a nation before Me forever." Thus says the Lord: "If heaven above can be measured, And the foundations of the earth searched out beneath, I will also cast off all the seed of Israel For all that they have done, says the Lord.
>
> —Jeremiah 31:35–37

As long as the sun, moon, and stars remain on their course, Israel is safe. If anybody can measure heaven and can search out the foundations of the earth, or if the sun leaves her axis and the earth, her orbit, and the stars fall, then—and only then—will Israel's safety be in jeopardy.

Attestations of God's favor on Israel may be found throughout Scripture: "Now to Abraham and his Seed were the promises made. He does not say, 'And to seeds,' as of many, but as of one, 'And to your Seed,' who is Christ" (Gal. 3:16); "By faith Abraham, when he was tested, offered up Isaac, and he who had received the promises offered up his only begotten son, of whom it was said, 'In Isaac your seed shall be called'" (Heb. 11:17–18).

Israel has been cast out into the nations and yet she survives. A Jewish anthem expresses the continual hope of Israelites to return to the home God gave them:

> As long as deep within the heart
> The Jewish soul is warm
> And toward the edges of the east
> An eye to Zion looks
> Our hope is not yet lost,
> The hope of two thousand years
> To be a free people in our own land
> In the land of Zion and Jerusalem.
> To be a free people in our own land
> In the land of Zion and Jerusalem.[1]

A miraculous phenomenon took place May 14, 1948. After 2,500 years without self-government and 1,800 years without a national home, Israel had every reason to be extinct. Yet on that day a historical phenomenon appeared:

a nation that had been dead suddenly came to life. It seems a direct fulfillment of Scripture: "For I will take you from among the nations, gather you out of all countries, and bring you into your own land" (Ez. 36:24).

Mark Twain penned these words in 1898:

> The Egyptian, the Babylonian and the Persian rose, filled the planet with sound and splendor, then faded to dream-stuff and passed away; the Greek and the Roman followed, and made a vast noise, and they are gone; other peoples have sprung up and held their torch high for a time, but it burned out, and they sit in twilight now, or have vanished. The Jew saw them all, beat them all, and is now what he always was, exhibiting no decadence, no infirmities of age, no weakening of his parts, no slowing of his energies, no dulling of his alert and aggressive mind. All things are mortal but the Jew; all other forces pass, but he remains.[2]

Do Twain's words not testify to the Word of the Lord given to Jeremiah so long ago?

The book of Joshua records the giving of the land to Israel.

> Moses My servant is dead. Now therefore, arise, go over this Jordan, you and all this people, to the land which I am giving to them—the children of Israel.... From the wilderness and this Lebanon as far as the great river, the River Euphrates, all the land of the Hittites, and to the Great Sea toward the going down of the sun, shall be your

> territory. . . . Be strong and of good courage, for to this people you shall divide as an inheritance the land which I swore to their fathers to give them. . . . Pass through the camp and command the people, saying, "Prepare provisions for yourselves, for within three days you will cross over this Jordan, to go in to possess the land which the Lord your God is giving you to possess."
>
> —Joshua 1:2, 4, 6, 11

> I have given you a land for which you did not labor, and cities which you did not build, and you dwell in them; you eat of the vineyards and olive groves which you did not plant.
>
> —Joshua 24:13

After the Israelites were delivered from Egypt, the Lord reaffirmed his covenant: "Then the Angel of the Lord came up from Gilgal to Bochim, and said: 'I led you up from Egypt and brought you to the land of which I swore to your fathers; and I said, "I will never break My covenant with you"'" (Judg. 2:1).

God gave the land to Israel. God's covenant with Abraham, Isaac, and Jacob is an everlasting covenant. The land God granted to Israel remains theirs as long as God's covenant remains, and God said it was forever.

One of the reasons for God's divine favor on America has been that America has been a blesser-nation to Israel. I began this chapter quoting God's promise to Israel that "I will bless those who bless you, I will curse him who curses you" (Gen 12:3). This covenant of blessings and curses remains in effect today. For the last fifteen years, America has blessed Israel with one hand and cursed her with the other hand. With one hand, America has voted in support of Israel in critical issues, and with the other hand, has pressured Israel to give up land for peace. In other words, Israel has been blackmailed into giving up land to keep the Palestinians from attacking them. But what if America turns from Israel?

There are five key facts that world leaders pressuring Israel have failed to recognize.

- God gave the land to Abraham and reaffirmed His covenant to Isaac and to Jacob (Gen. 28:13).
- God established the boundaries of the land given to Abraham (Gen. 15:18).
- God included the land in His covenant and said it is everlasting (Gen. 17:7). Therefore, the land belongs to Israel forever.
- Some interpret biblical prophecy to say that when Jesus, the Son of God, returns to Earth, He will return to the Mount of Olives facing Jerusalem (Zech. 14:4).
- Those who curse Israel in word or deed will be cursed by God (Gen. 12:3).

I am disappointed that American presidents have played key roles in pressuring Israel to give up land to maintain peace in the Middle East. This is not a Democrat or Republican issue. This is not an oil issue. This is a God issue, something He addressed in the Bible thousands of years ago.

He has kept His word and will continue to keep His word, both to Israel and to nations that bless or curse her. World leaders who support the ultimatum given to Israel to give up land to avoid being attacked are not only fighting Israel, but are fighting against God. They are not only stealing land from Israel, but are stealing the land that God gave to Israel; in effect, they are stealing from God.

It may seem that Israel stands alone in this situation, but I remind Israel of another battle long ago when a young lad, David, faced a nine-feet-tall giant named Goliath who seemed far superior and stronger. Of course, we know how that fight turned out. The same God that gave David the victory in the midst of daunting opposition has promised victory for Israel today. Israel should place their trust in God and tell the United Nations, "You come against us in the name of world government and in the name of the bullies that threaten us to rob Israel of what belongs to us: a land given to us thousands of years ago. But we stand against you in the name of the God who gave it to us. We will never give up the inheritance we received from Jehovah God!"

It grieves me that so many in America have joined the voices of the lynch mob that scream for Israel's blood in the name of peace. It also grieves me that the leaders of Israel retreat from this confrontation and continue to relinquish their land. Is there no one who will stand up for God? Is there no one who will proclaim what the Word of the Lord says? Is there no leader in America who will ask, how can we turn our backs on Israel and on the God of Israel, who is also the God of America, the One who has protected us for four hundred years? Will we stand by and watch as Israel retreats from her inheritance?

The Christian church should understand that Israel is the place of our heritage, our roots. *Charisma* magazine published an article by Robert Stearns on the importance of Israel. Stearns wrote, "Christianity did not form in a vacuum. Our faith was generated from a consecrated place—Israel—and a chosen people—the Jews. The gospel is a Jewish message about a Jewish Messiah given to Jewish disciples within a Jewish context. The Bible tells us that salvation is 'of the Jews' (John 4:22, NKJV) and that to them 'pertain the adoption, the glory, the covenants...and the promises; of whom are the fathers and from whom, according to the flesh, Christ came, who is over all, the eternally blessed God' (Rom. 9:4–5). To not understand where we have come from is to not be clear about who we are, where we are and where we are going."[3]

Is there no leader in Israel who will remind the world God gave that land to their fathers—Abraham, Isaac, and Jacob—and reaffirmed that covenant with King David? When Israel desired meat for food in the wilderness, Moses asked how meat could be provided for such a great multitude, since feeding them would require all the fish in the Red Sea. In response, God asked if His arm had been shortened. That same question can be asked today. Is the arm of God shortened such that He can no long deliver Israel and provide for them, forcing them to abandon the inheritance of our fathers?

Even in Israel, many are willing to appease those who seek her destruction by conceding land. Some public opinion polls reveal that 50 percent or more of Jews in Israel would trade land for peace.[4] Although more than a decade old, the following quote supports the notion that Israel herself is willing to give up land: "Recent developments in the Arab-Israeli peace process indicate that the Israeli Government has already made the choice and is ready to exchange land for peace."[5] American Jews have likewise been willing to secure peace at the cost of giving up land. Following the 1993 Oslo Accords, 68 percent supported conceding land for peace.[6]

Support for the exchange of land for peace no doubt varies depending on the mood of the times, frequency and severity of terrorist attacks against Israel, and the politics within and outside of Israel. For example, following a series of Palestinian terrorist attacks against Israel in 2000, many Jews in Israel who had believed strongly in negotiation to achieve peace changed their minds. A 2002 newspaper article says, "In Israel... 'right' usually means approaching negotiations with suspicion and supporting settlements in the disputed lands. 'Left' means a good-hearted eagerness to negotiate with the Palestinians, an attitude that may be revived eventually but has now become so unpopular that it seems almost quaint."[7]

Perhaps what is more constant is the division of Jews into distinct camps. There are those in Israel who believe concessions are a necessary part of negotiations. Opposing these concessions are individuals who either believe that the land is "in accordance with God's plan for the Jewish people and mankind"[8] or those who claim "the land of the ancient Hebrew commonwealths as a national birthright."[9] There are differences in the opinions of Jews living in America, too: "At the core of the problem is the split in U.S. Jewry between the more secularized element in the community, who define their Judaism through a liberal-universalistic religiosity, and the hard core, composed of nationalist and the Orthodox,"[10] the former more readily supporting trading land, the latter more opposed.

Why do the world's governments clamor for Israel to surrender its land? Do others have a greater claim? In *Jerusalem Countdown*, John Hagee writes, "Arabs began to repopulate the land only after the Jews reclaimed it and the land had begun to prosper. No nation in the region has a longer-standing historic claim to the land than Israel. Saudi Arabia was not created until 1913; Lebanon, 1920; Iraq, 1932; Syria, 1941; Jordan, 1946; and Kuwait, 1961."[11] When Nehemiah started rebuilding the city of Jerusalem, an Arab, an Ammonite, and a Horonite laughed at him. He replied, "The God of heaven Himself will prosper us; therefore we His servants will arise and build, but you have no heritage or right or memorial in Jerusalem" (Neh. 2:20).

I repeat: nations that pressure Israel into giving up the land God gave to them are stealing from God. God gave the land to Israel forever. God Himself became the arbiter, protector, and power of attorney in this dispute. There are no negotiations.

America will bear the judgment of God by being party to the "land for peace" program. This exchange program reminds me of the promises of underworld and mafia leaders who say, "If you pay me, then I won't hurt you." The world bullies and Israel concedes, but Israel will never be at peace until the Prince of Peace returns to establish His kingdom and fulfill the promise to King David.

Hear the words of the prophet Zechariah:

> And it shall happen in that day that I will make Jerusalem a very heavy stone for all peoples; all who would heave it away will surely be cut in

> pieces, though all nations of the earth are gathered against it.... It shall be in that day that I will seek to destroy all the nations that come against Jerusalem.
>
> —Zechariah 12:3, 9

John McTernan and Bill Koenig, in their book *Israel: The Blessing or the Curse*, detail a long list of critical dates and events of disasters that struck America each time official meetings were set up to consummate agreements by which Israel would relinquish land for peace.[12] Is this mere coincidence, or judgment? Pastor John Hagee declares that "Jerusalem is the heart of Israel. There are voices now calling for the sacred city to be shared as a part of the Roadmap for Peace in the Middle East. Let it be known to all men far and near, the city of Jerusalem is not up for negotiation with anyone at any time for any reason in the future. It has been and shall always be the eternal and undivided capital of the State of Israel."[13] I concur with Pastor Hagee. The ownership and occupancy of Jerusalem are not negotiable. It will be the site for the Lord's return when He returns to set up His kingdom.

Note this chilling description of current events in Israel:

> Jewish settlers were dragged from homes and synagogues amid tears and bitterness as Israeli troops Wednesday completed the forced evacuation of seven of 21 settlements in the Gaza Strip.... "There are no words to describe this feeling. There is no psychologist in the world who could describe it", said a tearful soldier who encountered religious Jews in Morag settlement who wanted him to

> pray with them.... The United Nations says that Israeli settlements are illegal under international law, a determination that Israel disputes. The United States calls them an obstacle to peace in the Middle East.[14]

The United States' stance in Israeli-Palestinian politics too closely resembles response of Neville Chamberlain when he signed off on Hitler's aggression.

I confess I know little about foreign policy, but I do know something about the Bible. The Bible is very plain about the land of Israel. America is in trouble when she pressures Israel to give up land God has given them.

We don't need men in leadership who are good politicians; we need politicians who are good men and who will stand up for what is right. Too many politicians are guilty of doing what is politically correct instead of what is simply correct.

Political and financial pressures have caused American leaders and merchants to take the road of least resistance, whether in foreign policy or in the market place in America. Are Christians in America also going to take this easy path? Will apathy overrule zeal? Will comfort trump action? Will the desire for security lead to the willing loss of liberty?

Chapter 10
CHRISTIAN APATHY

Our lives begin to end the day we become silent about things that matter.[1]
—Dr. Martin Luther King, Jr.

APATHY IS NOT AN APPROPRIATE RESPONSE TO crisis situations. When your religious freedom is stripped away and attempts are made to regulate your worship, it is not the correct response to ignore what is happening.

Why have Christians been silent? Robert Stearns theorizes that "a spiritually complacent Western church seems unaware or in denial regarding the twin threats to the future of Western civilization—radical Islam and secular humanism."[2]

Complacency and ease are serious threats to our ability to mount the proper response. Bill Kristol writes regarding American political conservatives, "It's not easy to rally a comfortable and commercial people to assume the responsibilities of a great power. It's not easy to defend excellence in an egalitarian age. It's not easy to encourage self-reliance in the era of the welfare state. It's not easy to make the case for the traditional virtues in the face of the seductions of liberation, or to speak of duties in a world of rights and of honor in a nation pursuing pleasure."[3] No, it is not easy, but we must nevertheless cast off our lethargy and shake ourselves from our slumber if we are to overcome the assaults on our freedom.

Sometimes, the issue isn't complacency: it's complicity. Many religious leaders work with secular humanists—many are humanists themselves—to enable their agenda. Andrew Bonar said long ago, "I looked for the church and found it in the world. I looked for the world and found it in the church."[4]

In an article in *Charisma* magazine, J. Lee Grady profiles two ministers in Russia: Pastor Henry Madava of the 6,500-member Victory Christian Church in Kiev, Ukraine; and Pastor Sunday Adelaja, a Nigerian, who leads a twenty-five-thousand-member congregation, the Embassy of God, also in Kiev. Grady writes, "Both Madava, 40, and Adelaja, 38, are concerned about what they call a 'superstar syndrome' that is spreading from the United States to churches around the world. It seduces leaders to become arrogant and greedy. When Adelaja hears about the glamorous lifestyle of some American ministers, he gets a puzzled look on his face. 'Is this a virus?' he asks."[5]

Grady quotes Madava regarding the American church. "Many leaders in America have received the anointing but they have become clouds without water."[6]

Christian leaders have a heavy responsibility to keep the people informed and aware.

> But if the watchman sees the sword coming and does not blow the trumpet, and the people are not warned, and the sword comes and takes any person from among them, he is taken away in his iniquity; but his blood I will require at the watchman's hand.
>
> —EZEKIEL 33:6

> For if you remain completely silent at this time, relief and deliverance will arise for the Jews from another place, but you and your father's house will perish. Yet who knows whether you have come to the kingdom for such a time as this?
>
> —Esther 4:14

If those called of God to speak His Word remain silent and allow His children to perish, there will be consequences. God will accomplish his divine plan, but what is the cost of silence? The Word clearly teaches that ministers, or "watchmen," are held responsible for warning the people regarding the coming judgment. Those with the responsibility of caring for the flock are no doubt "brought to the kingdom for such a time as this." The only question that remains is, how will we respond?

It is time for the people of God to understand that the Word demands that we are to be a holy nation, just as each individual is called to holiness. God is more interested in what we *are* than what we *do* because what we are dictates what we do. We are to be like Him and we are to do His will.

Some may respond to this charge by saying that America is a secular nation, not a theocracy. I am not calling for a theocracy until Jesus Himself establishes His kingdom. I am calling, however, for Christians to take seriously the responsibility laid on them to be like Christ, to be holy as He is holy, and to do the work of Christ. And I am calling for Christians to make their voices heard, to resist the confiscation of rights given by God, and to let the world know in uncertain terms that we will no longer tolerate the offenses tossed our way.

Martin Luther King, Jr., said, "History will not judge this time by the viciousness of our enemies so much as it will by the silence of our friends."[7] Lutheran pastor Martin Niemöeller, upon his liberation from Dachau concentration camp, reportedly expressed a similar thought: "In Germany, when the Nazis came for the Communists, I didn't speak up because I wasn't a Communist. Then they came for the trade unionists, but I said nothing because I wasn't a trade unionist. Then they came for the Catholics, and I kept quiet because I wasn't a Catholic. Later they came for the Jews, but I wasn't a Jew so I didn't say a word. Then, they came for me, and by that time there was no one left to speak up for me."[8]

I love Elizabeth Barrett Browning's beautiful words:

> Earth's crammed with heaven,
> And every common bush afire with God;
> But only he who sees, takes off his shoes,
> The rest sit around and pluck blackberries.[9]

Those blinded to the dangers threatening America, instead of seeing the bush on fire, are busy plucking blackberries. We must stand up and be counted. We must not be intimidated by those who seek to destroy our great country or who desire to rob us of freedom. We must say with Joshua, "But as for me and my house, we will serve the LORD" (Josh. 24:15).

America should be offended by the actions of the ACLU, atheists, activist judges, and political leaders, especially those intended to ban worship or prayer in the name of Jesus on government and public property. Our acquiescence to this terrible offense should be an embarrassment to the people of God.

David Limbaugh recounts the story of a school teacher in a Denver elementary school who was ordered to remove his Bible from the library and to remove his personal Bible from his desk, where he kept it "to read during silent time.... School officials...prohibited the teacher from reading it and made him hide it during the school day, even though he never read from it to his students."[10] Are these school officials wiser than Abraham Lincoln, who said this about the Bible:

> In regard to this Great Book, I have but to say, it is the best gift God has given to man. All the good the Savior gave to the world was communicated through this book. But for it we could not know right from wrong. All things most desirable for man's welfare, here and hereafter, are to be found portrayed in it.[11]

Yet, school officials, politicians, judges, even the Supreme Court, have thrown it into the trashcan. In generations past, who would believe that American judges would or could deny any person the right to read the Bible or to pray in the name of Jesus? There is no judge, legislator, or power in America with the authority to deny anyone the right to pray in the name of Jesus. Nonetheless, when governmental abuse raises its ugly head, we are silent.

If today it is a crime to speak the name of Jesus in a high school or state Senate meeting, will it be a crime tomorrow to speak the name of Jesus on the public airwaves? Will chaplains be drummed out of military service? By whose authority do judges derive the right to dictate to an American citizen whom he or she can publicly worship? Certainly not the Constitution. These judges, politicians, and organizations raise their voices against freedom. But where are the voices of Christians crying out to right these wrongs? Where is the weeping over the losses of our freedom of speech and freedom of religion? Where are the ministers and churches weeping over America as Jesus wept over Jerusalem in Luke 19:41?

Too often, businesses and politicians pander to the people who seek to deny American freedom. At the same time, many Christians too readily support businesses that support anti-Christian, anti-American groups. This needs to stop. There are small signs that Christians have had enough of suffering abuses. For example, in recent years department stores began avoiding the use of the word *Christmas* in advertisements. Instead, they used the word *holiday*. Christmas trees were renamed "holiday trees" and choruses of "Merry Christmas" were replaced by the greeting, "Happy holidays." Christmas carols were banned from schools and nativity scenes banned from government properties. But Christians fought back successfully. Backlash from critical shoppers influenced many stores to bring back words related to Christmas.[12] This is a small example, but it shows that when Christians unify our voices they can affect the behavior of those who depend on us.

Coupled with the deep-seated secular humanism that has infiltrated our society is an equally deep-seated hypocrisy. When Judge Samuel Kent was reprimanded by the judicial council of the Fifth U.S. Circuit Court of Appeals for alleged sexual harassment, a four-month leave of absence was imposed on the judge.[13] This is more leniency than Judge Kent was willing to give high school students for speaking Jesus' name at their graduation. Since when is speaking the name of Jesus a more serious crime than sexual harassment?[14]

What message is America's judiciary sending if Judge Edward Cashman can sentence a man to a mere sixty days in prison for raping a seven-year-old girl repeatedly over a period of years, but Judge Kent may threaten to sentence teenagers to six months in prison for speaking the name of Jesus in a high school graduation service? Since when does mentioning the name of Jesus merit a punishment three times more severe than that of a serial child rapist?

For those trying to bury Jesus, someone should tell them it's already been tried—two thousand years ago—but on the third day, *He rose again!* Neither Herod, nor Pilate, nor the Roman army, nor those who lied about Him, nor the devil, nor demons, nor hell itself could keep him in the grave. The Supreme Court of the United States can't bury Him. The ACLU can't bury Him. Politicians can't bury Him. Atheists can't bury Him. Jesus declared, "I am He who lives, and was dead, and behold, I am alive forevermore. Amen. And I have the keys of Hades and of Death" (Rev. 1:18).

The reason we pray in the name of Jesus is because He is the person and object of our worship. God the Father Himself named His son Jesus: "And she will bring forth a Son, and you shall call His name JESUS, for He will save His people from their sins" (Matt. 1:21).

There is power in His name.

> And whatever you ask in My name, that I will do, that the Father may be glorified in the Son. If you ask anything in My name, I will do it.
>
> —John 14:13–14

> Nor is there salvation in any other, for there is no other name under heaven given among men by which we must be saved.
>
> —ACTS 4:12

> And these signs will follow those who believe: In My name they will cast out demons; they will speak with new tongues; they will take up serpents; and if they drink anything deadly, it will by no means hurt them; they will lay hands on the sick, and they will recover.
>
> —MARK 16:17–18

All of these verses explain why the devil, atheists, devil worshipers, secular humanists, and activist judges hate His name—it is a source of power infinitely greater than they are.

On the other hand, the founding fathers understood very well the words of the Apostles to the rulers and religious leaders of their day: "But Peter and John answered and said to them, 'Whether it is right in the sight of God to listen to you more than to God, you judge'" (Acts 4:19). There is coming a day when all the anti-God, anti-Christian, anti-Jesus activists and judges will bow before Jesus Himself, as prophesied in Philippians 2:9–11: "Therefore God also has highly exalted Him and given Him the name which is above every name, that at the name of Jesus every knee should bow, of those in heaven, and of those on earth, and of those under the earth, and that every tongue should confess that Jesus Christ is Lord, to the glory of God the Father."

Our forefathers understood the importance of recognizing and defending the sovereignty of Christ and the power of His name, even in the face of suffering. Their stories and sacrifices are not so different from that of the early apostles who experienced persecution for refusing to keep their faith quiet: "And when they had called for the apostles and beaten them, they commanded that they should not speak in the name of Jesus, and let them go. So they departed from the presence of the council, rejoicing that they were counted worthy to suffer shame for His name" (Acts 5:40–41). Because of the founders' actions, faith, and sacrifice, America has been a nation divinely favored of God. It has correctly been designated as a Christian nation for nearly two hundred years.

Now, because of the actions of politicians, judges, and secular humanists, we have officially been designated a non-Christian nation. We have allowed activist judges to rob us and steal our birthright of spiritual freedom. Are we as Christians to remain silent? Or are we to fight as Washington and Franklin and Adams fought? Are we to resist with the firm understanding of the Constitution and the firm reliance upon Scripture?

In the most critical time in the life of Jesus upon Earth, He prayed in the Garden of Gethsemane. His soul was sorrowful unto death and His sweat as great drops of blood. But where were His disciples? They were asleep. (See Matthew 26:43, 45.) Jesus' words to His disciples are appropriate to us today: "Are you still sleeping and resting? Behold, the hour is at hand, and the Son of Man is being betrayed into the hands of sinners" (Matt. 26:45).

While Jesus is attacked in the courts, the media, the marketplace, schools, and political forums, the church is asleep, "for their eyes are heavy" (Matt. 26:43). Will His disciples—will you, will I—sleep once again when Jesus needs His people to be vigilant? Will He depend on us to bring renewal to the church and revival to the land, only to find us content in slumber?

Only you can decide for yourself, but my answer will be the same as Joshua's: "As for me and my house, we will serve the LORD" (Josh. 24:15).

Chapter 11
DIVINE JUDGMENT

Nations, like individuals are
punished for their transgressions.[1]
—Ulysses S. Grant

CHRISTIANS HAVE LARGELY REMAINED SILENT while organizations and individuals have taken measures to remove God and the worship of Him from public expression. Because of these actions and because of Christian inaction, what was once divine favor has turned to divine judgment.

As we sit silent, the world suffers. As we satiate ourselves with pleasure rather than with earnest desire to confront evil and turn the world to God, judgment falls: "The wicked shall be turned into hell, And all the nations that forget God" (Ps. 9:17). Judgment falls upon us because of our silence, because of our apathy, because of our comfort zone, and because we are more interested in "business as usual." Judgment falls upon us because we are more interested in electing politicians who can make the biggest promises and who can construct the largest pork barrels than we are about the favor of God. We are more interested in what we can receive than what we can do to bring revival to our country and renewal to the body of Christ. We are more interested in being entertained than being the active, responsible participants described in the phrase "government by the people."

Consequences follow the rejection of God: "Woe to those who decree unrighteous decrees, Who write misfortune, Which they have prescribed" (Isa. 10:1). The great patriot Patrick Henry addressed the Virginia Convention on June 5, 1788, with these words: "[If] our descendants be worthy the name of Americans, they will preserve and hand down to their latest posterity, the transactions of the present times."[2] *We are that posterity!* Have we preserved the godly spirit of liberty our forefathers fought for? Do we have the courage and bravery to pass on to our posterity the values received from those who have waged war to preserve freedom?

If not, judgment will fall upon us because we build bigger barns and ignore the impoverished at our gates begging bread.

If not, judgment will fall upon us because we are lovers of pleasure more than lovers of God.

If not, judgment will fall upon us because we worship at the shrines of athletes, movie idols, entertainers, and the wealthy more than we worship God. (For what other reason do we pay entertainers and athletes exorbitant salaries while paying those who educate our children and protect our nation very little?)

If not, judgment will fall on us because we see the wounded and robbed men and women lying by the roadside, and pass by on the other side. We leave good deeds to others, but fail to accept responsibility ourselves.

If not, judgment will fall on us because we seek to please man rather than to please God. We trust in political connections rather than in a divine connection. We forget that God is our source, our provider, our protector, and our deliverer.

If not, judgment will fall on us because we are silent when

the rabble-rousers denounce the God of Glory because we don't want to appear to be radical.

God is a longsuffering God, but His longsuffering will come to an end. America has enjoyed God's divine favor for a long time, but now she is rejecting God. I believe God is removing His umbrella of protection.

Many believe the Civil War was the worst period in American history. Why did it happen? Several factors contributed to war breaking out and pitting North against South, neighbor against neighbor, and brother against brother; but there was an insidious sin in the soul of this young country: slavery. Some people even today try to twist the Bible to say that the apostle Paul was not opposed to slavery because of his admonitions to Onesimus, a runaway slave, to return to his master. But Paul was not addressing the issue of slavery; he was addressing the issue of relationships. He refers to Onesimus as "my son" (Philem. 1:10). Although he asked Onesimus, his convert, to return to Philemon, he also asked Philemon to receive his runaway slave as he would receive Paul if he were there physically. He asked Philemon to receive Onesimus "no longer as a slave but more than a slave—a beloved brother" (v. 16). Paul taught that the ground is level at the foot of the cross.

Christians prior to the Civil War should have realized this critical lesson. Many did, but some did not. Non-Christians, too, forgot lessons they should have known. I believe this acceptance and perpetration of slavery caused God to remove His favor. God allowed America to suffer the consequences of her sin. He gave us the opportunity to repent. Is it a coincidence that immediately prior to the Civil War a powerful revival movement swept America? Did this great revival prepare America to repent and to accept the consequences of prior sin? This revival, characterized by prayer, had significant positive consequences for America (and other countries to which it spread). "The revival of 1859 had similar effects in the North and the South, and may have prepared many Americans spiritually to survive the horrors of the war that broke out a few years later. The awakening continued into the Civil War period, a great revival occurring in the Southern armies in 1863–64."[3] Even in sin, God did not quit loving America. He still had a destiny for her. He removed the hedge, but did not forsake her. When the wrong was righted, when the nation repented, He preserved the Union. America then continued on her divinely favored course. God had a plan of greatness for America.

It is not necessary that God rain judgment down upon America. If He simply removes His protection, America will reap the consequences of her unbelief and rebellion.

On *The Early Show* author and speaker Anne Graham, the daughter of Billy Graham, said this about God allowing disasters such as Hurricane Katrina to befall America: "I believe God is deeply saddened by this, just as we are. But for years we've been telling God to get out of our schools, to get out of our government and to get out of our lives. Being the gentleman that He is, I believe that He has calmly backed out. How can we expect God to give us His blessing and His protection if we demand He leave us alone?"[4] I agree. God does not need to send natural or man-made disasters as retribution. Rejected, all He need do is allow us to receive the consequences of our actions without His "superintending Providence."[5] If we face the consequences of our action and inaction, the blame is not on God, but rather on America.

Voices Crying in the Wilderness

> "So I sought for a man among them who would make a wall, and stand in the gap before Me on behalf of the land, that I should not destroy it; but I found no one. Therefore I have poured out My indignation on them; I have consumed them with the fire of My wrath; and I have recompensed their deeds on their own heads," says the Lord GOD.
>
> —EZEKIEL 22:30–31

God seeks for those—sometimes, simply for one—who will stand in the gap. Who will plead for America? Where is today's Moses, who pleaded with God to spare Israel in the wilderness?

> Then Moses returned to the LORD and said, "Oh, these people have committed a great sin, and have made for themselves a god of gold! Yet now, if You will forgive their sin—but if not, I pray, blot me out of Your book which You have written.
>
> —EXODUS 32:31–32

Where is today's Abraham, who interceded for the city of Sodom and asked God if He would spare Sodom if there were ten righteous found in the city? God listened and said, "I will not destroy it for the sake of ten" (Gen. 18:32).

Where is today's apostle Paul who will beg God for "my countrymen according to the flesh" (Rom. 9:3)? Earlier in the same verse, Paul said, "For I could wish that I myself were accursed from Christ for my brethren."

I thank God for the voices crying in the wilderness, people

like John Hagee, Roy Moore, Justice Antonin Scalias, Robert Bork, Donald Wildmon, Hal Lindsey, Jay Sekulow, Rick Scarborough, and many more. A few voices rise, inviting ridicule but nevertheless speaking truth, while most remain silent.

When God removes His hedge of protection, His divine favor, then we are vulnerable to the attacks of our enemies. God assured David and the people of Israel that their military strength resided in Him, not in numbers, and forbade the king to take up a census. When King David sinned against God by numbering the people, God pronounced judgment upon David. Through the prophet Gad, God gave David three choices: to endure seven years of famine, fleeing before his enemies for three months, or suffering three days of pestilence in the land. David responded, "I am in great distress. Please let us fall into the hand of the LORD, for His mercies are great; but do not let me fall into the hand of man" (2 Sam. 24:14).

In Romans, the apostle Paul identified sin and unbelief as the reason why God had scattered the Jews throughout the nations of the world. He called Israel the natural branches and the church, the body of Christ, as the wild olive branches that had to be grafted in to the natural tree. (See Romans 11:17–24.) Israel was the chosen of God, but God did not withhold His judgment when Israel sinned and rejected Jesus, His Son. Paul also issued a warning to the church that they were not immune to the judgment of God when they sinned: "For if God did not spare the natural branches, He may not spare you either" (Rom. 11:21). Paul continued, "For if you were cut out of the olive tree which is wild by nature, and were grafted contrary to nature into a cultivated olive tree, how much more will these, who are natural branches, be grafted into their own olive tree?" (v. 24).

Today we may ask, if God chastised Israel—the good olive tree, the covenant nation—for their sins, will He spare America, which also stands guilty? Unless there is genuine repentance in America and the nation returns to the God of its birth, judgment will surely fall. Without God's protection, America will fall into the hands of her enemies or into some other form of judgment.

Chapter 12

RETURN TO GOD'S DESTINY

SECOND CHRONICLES 7:13 DESCRIBES GOD'S WORD of judgment on His people: "When I shut up heaven and there is no rain, or command the locusts to devour the land, or send pestilence among My people." In the next verse, hear the remedy God offers: "If My people who are called by My name will humble themselves, and pray and seek My face, and turn from their wicked ways, then I will hear from heaven, and will forgive their sin and heal their land" (v. 14). God pronounced judgment upon the great city of Nineveh of 120,000 people, but when Jonah preached to them and warned them, they repented and turned to God. Jonah 3:10 says, "Then God saw their works, that they turned from their evil way; and God relented from the disaster that He had said He would bring upon them, and He did not do it."

God always prepares a way of escape for those who will accept it. Apostles, prophets, pastors, evangelists, teachers, and others are warning people to turn to God. Christians today need to proclaim with the prophet Amos, "But let justice run down like water, And righteousness like a mighty stream" (Amos 5:24). If God has ever needed a true prophet to stand up and warn a nation of what is about to come upon this earth, it is today. Hear the instruction of Leonard Ravenhill:

> Most do not need more light, we need more obedience—a month of heart-searching, a month of doing what Joel says: sanctify a fast, call a solemn assembly, with the priests and ministers weeping between the altar and the doorposts; with prostrate preachers acknowledging their spiritual bankruptcy and lack of love for souls, for such the Holy Word says, 'Wail, you who minister before the altar; Come, lie all night in sackcloth, You who minister to my God' (Joel 1:13). This is God's formula for revival. Is He bound to honor anything less than this?[1]

What is God's plan for America? America has been a land favored by God since its inception because of its future role in world evangelism, its freedom of speech, her civil liberties and freedom of religion, and because she would be a haven and refuge for the disenfranchised around the world. The founding fathers established the young nation under God. Central to this religious freedom was the First Amendment statement that Congress would make no law establishing any religion. America became the bastion for the religiously persecuted. All citizens who desire to worship can do so according to his or her conscience without fear of reprisal from the state. Sing "America the Beautiful" and listen to the refrain "God shed His grace on thee," sing "The Star-Spangled Banner" and hear the description of America as "the land of the free," or sing "God Bless America" and feel your heart swell with pride at the phrase "my home sweet home."

The great awakenings of the last three centuries share certain characteristics. In all of them, people were focused on intercessory prayer, anointed preaching, strong witnessing by the laity, praise and worship, passion for unconverted people, courage and commitment to stand against fierce opposition, the call to repentance and holiness, and benevolence toward the poor and unfortunate.

In *History of the Work of Redemption*, Jonathan Edwards wrote that whenever true religions seemed to be on the verge of extinction, "God granted a revival, and sent some angel, or raised up some eminent person, to be an instrument of their reformation."[2] In the early 1700s, God used the Moravian community to spark an awakening on two continents. God used men such as Jonathan Edwards, George Whitfield, Charles Wesley, and others to bring about the Great Awakening. God used men such as Charles Finney and Peter Cartwright to ignite the Second Great Awakening in the early 1800s. Laymen were used to flame the fire of the prayer revival in the mid-nineteenth century. The Holiness Revival followed in the late 1800s and was a prelude to the Pentecostal Awakening. God started the Pentecostal Awakening from the Shearer school house near Murphy, North Carolina; a Bible school in Topeka, Kansas; in Houston, Texas; in the great Azusa Street revival in Los Angeles, California; and in the countries of Wales and Korea.

Regardless of whether the revival began in a country schoolhouse or a thriving metropolis, the experiences and method were the same: a powerful, dynamic of renewal that began with fervent intercessory prayer.

Even so, each awakening was unique and bore the distinctive stamp of the Holy Spirit's unction and direction. Charles Finney wrote, "When he (God) has found that a certain mode has lost its influence by having become a form, he brings up some new measure, which will break in upon their lazy habits, and wake up a slumbering church."[3]

What are the elements necessary to bring a new awakening? Let's look to the efforts that preceded the Great Awakening and other renewals in the past. Gerald McDermott summarizes renewal movements:

> Revivals were preceded by corporate prayer. Early in the century it had become an evangelical truism that revival usually followed God's outpouring of a spirit of intercession for revival.... The 18th-century revivals produced several networks of corporate prayer for the spiritual renewal of the world.... revival preachers in the 18th century explicitly denounced "legalistic" and "rationalist" preaching that taught "mere morality." In contrast, they emphasized justification by faith in the atoning death of Christ.... Revivalists preached at non-traditional times in non-traditional places.... Wesley preached in jails to prisoners, in inns to wayfarers, and on vessels to passengers crossing to Ireland.[4]

While the circumstances differ today, the strategy remains the same: find hurting people wherever they are and minister to them. We must discover and identify new channels, new forums, and new methods and strategies to do this, rather than limit ourselves to the traditional church buildings as the only place of sharing the good news of Jesus Christ.

Now, in the early years of a new millennium, it is America that needs revival. Freedom is losing ground every day. Values and ethics are foreign to our classrooms. Children grow up without a strong foundation in right and wrong, respect and altruism, and, yes, Christian love. The sending nation has become the receiving nation. America needs spiritual renewal in order to return to God's plan for the nation.

The lack of ethics in the ranks of government officials, businessmen, and clergy reveal the devastating effects of a country adrift without godly restraints. Instead of the church influencing society, the church becomes corrupt from society's influence. The answer is *revival*, spiritual renewal.

We face a critical time in American history, and this nation must experience renewal in the church and revival in all society in order to survive. The strength of America is the faith and prayers of Christian people. We must have renewal for the future of our children and grandchildren. We are reaping the harvest of a generation that has grown up without the benefits of the Bible and prayer. We must have renewal for divine favor to be restored to America.

The church steeples that dapple the American landscape comprise a great symbol of God's protection. But steeples are not enough. There must be fervent, intercessory prayer and genuine praise and worship inside the buildings those steeples adorn. We must have renewal for God to occupy His place of sovereignty in our nation and Jesus to occupy His place as Lord over our lives and government. We must have renewal because of the soon coming of Jesus Christ to remove His church from a world that has lost its way. Renowned Pastor W. A. Criswell writes, "By the decree of the Lord God Almighty, there is a day, there is an hour, there is a moment, there is an elected time when the angel shall sound and the kingdoms of this world shall become the kingdoms of our God and of His Christ."[5]

It is time for the body of Christ to put aside differences and hair-splitting over trivial issues. The church must join hands and accept one another as brothers and sisters in Christ. In so doing, the church will fulfill the prayer of Jesus when He prayed to the Father to make us one (John 17:22).

God has always used revival—whether formal or informal, preacher-based or layperson-initiated—to bring an awakening and renewal to His people. The history of humankind has followed a cycle of sin, suffering, supplication, deliverance, and renewal. God brought the earth out of chaos by renewal. He called Abraham out of heathenism to a covenant with Himself. He called Israel out of Egypt to a mountain of fire to worship Him. The history of the six judges in the book of Judges is really a history of six revivals. The preaching of John the Baptist on repentance brought revival to Israel and prepared the way for the coming Savior. Jesus Christ, the Messiah, came into the world to bring the greatest revival in the history of humankind.

Although God has touched many lives through prayer and revival, there has never been a successful coordination of all Christian groups. Never have all denominations, independents, evangelicals, fundamentalists, Pentecostals, and Charismatics worked together to institute a prayer plan to bring revival to America. Every member of the body of Christ has a responsibility to fan the flickering flames of revival until they burst into a raging forest fire that sweeps across America and burns out the dross and apathy. It is time for the American people to return to God and to their destiny as a nation.

The spiritual temperature is once again low in America. We need people that will pray diligently and witnesses to stand in the gap and make up a spiritual barrier of protection so that once again renewal and spiritual awakening will be sparked in America. We must be open to whatever methods God chooses to use to bring about the pre-Rapture awakening. I believe God has chosen the method of unity and prayer to bring about this great renewal.

Gerald McDermott says:

> New ways of singing . . . contributed to the emotionalism of 18th-century revivals. . . . Revival leaders often faced fierce opposition. . . . Wesley often had rocks thrown at him. . . . Edwards was hounded by liberal detractors in the press. . . . Revivals usually resulted in concern for the poor and unfortunate. . . . [Revival] comes only by the sovereign work of the Holy Spirit. We can do nothing to ensure such a work, but we can, and should, join with others to pray for an outpouring of the Spirit of God.[6]

Though McDermott's article is pointed at American evangelicals of the 1990s, I would add that these lessons should also be learned in the new millennium. As McDermott says, "Genuine spiritual renewal, if sufficiently deep and powerful, can do more to transform culture than political action can."[7]

Prayer

The history of the church has followed a cycle of spiritual coldness, compromise, repentance, forgiveness, and revival. Today, the church is again in a state of need for revival. What brings revival? Prayer! Prayer, indeed, changes things. Prayer offers greater protection than any antimissile system. Prayer is more powerful than any SDI defense system. It is prayer that has moved God again and again to intervene on behalf of America. When the church prays, America will repent. When America repents, revival will sweep across this nation. Then, America will awaken.

Prayer bears the fruit of godly sorrow for sin and influences the sinner to repent. Repentance bears the fruit of forgiveness and the joy of having one's sins forgiven. The greatest chapter in the Bible on repentance is Psalm 51. Notice the repentant spirit of David as he prayed for God's forgiveness.

> Have mercy upon me, O God....Blot out my transgressions. Wash me thoroughly from my iniquity, And cleanse me from my sin....Purge me with hyssop, and I shall be clean; Wash me, and I shall be whiter than snow. Make me hear joy and gladness, That the bones You have broken may rejoice. Hide Your face from my sins, And blot out all my iniquities. Create in me a clean heart, O God, And renew a steadfast spirit within me. Do not cast me away from Your presence, And do not take Your Holy Spirit from me. Restore to me the joy of Your salvation, And uphold me by Your generous Spirit. Then I will teach transgressors Your ways, And sinners shall be converted to You. Deliver me from bloodshed, O God.
>
> —Psalm 51:1, 7–14

William Morley Punshon, a nineteenth-century English Wesleyan minister, said, "Cowardice asks, 'Is it safe?' Expediency asks, 'Is it politic?' Vanity asks, 'Is it popular?' but Conscience asks, 'Is it right?'"[8] Dr. Martin Luther King, Jr., a great orator and champion of freedom, quoted Punshon before adding, "And there comes a time when one must take a position that is neither safe nor politic nor popular; but he must do it because Conscience tells him it is right."[9]

Reverend Wright, from the Central Christian Church in Wichita, Kansas, was asked to pray before the beginning of the new session of the Kansas House of Representatives in 1996. He prayed:

> Heavenly Father, we come before you today to ask Your forgiveness and to seek Your direction and guidance. We know Your Word says 'Woe to those who call evil good,' but that is exactly what we have done. We have lost our spiritual equilibrium and reversed our values. We confess that. We have ridiculed the absolute truth of Your Word and called it Pluralism. We have worshipped other gods and called it multiculturalism. We have endorsed perversion and called it alternative lifestyle. We have exploited the poor and called it the lottery. We have rewarded laziness and called it welfare. We have killed our unborn and called it choice. We have shot abortionists and called it justifiable. We have neglected to discipline our children and called it building self-esteem. We have abused power and called it politics. We have coveted our neighbor's possessions and called it ambition. We have polluted the air with profanity and pornography and called it freedom of expression. We have ridiculed the time-honored values of our forefathers and called it enlightenment. Search us, Oh, God, and know our hearts today; cleanse us from every sin and set us free.[10]

One legislator walked out during the prayer in protest. Three others spoke against his prayer, and one labeled the prayer a "message of intolerance." But many people understood: Christians, ministers and layperson alike, must speak the truth no matter the consequence. America needs more pastors like Reverend Joe Wright who will stand for God in places where the pressure builds to play to the crowd and to be politically correct.

One of the most encouraging articles I have read in a long time is a newspaper account of high school students in Russell Springs, Kentucky. After a federal judge blocked the high school from including prayers in its graduation ceremony, the students from the graduating class of 2006 took matters into their own hands. During the opening remarks, the students interrupted the principal's comments by reciting the Lord's Prayer. The crowd gave the students a standing ovation. A judge had banned prayers from the ceremony, but the students prayed anyway. "[Senior] Megan Chapman told the crowd that God had guided her since childhood. She was interrupted repeatedly by cheering as she urged her classmates to trust God as they go through life."[11] The decision of the federal judge was in response to a lawsuit filed by the American Civil Liberties Union on behalf of a single, unidentified student at the Russell County High School. Thank God for Russell County High School graduating seniors who were brave enough and courageous enough to take a stand for God. May their names be recorded in God's record book that they were counted worthy to represent Him to the entire world!

You and I can also make a difference. We need to follow the examples of these courageous young people. We can stand

and be counted. We can pray for our leaders who are under attack by the enemies of freedom. We can be resolved not to find excuses to stay home on election day. We can speak out on the issues and change the laws that threaten our liberties at the ballot box. We can elect God-fearing Christian men and women who believe the Bible; who are people of prayer; and who live the Christian life, loving God with a whole heart and loving our neighbors as ourselves. We can pray for our nation every day. We can commit to the building of the kingdom of God rather than building our own kingdoms and empires. Revival will come through prayer; but we also need men and women to stand their ground, to reject the secular humanism that perverts the Constitution, and to make their voices heard.

It is time for the people of God to ask themselves, is it right to keep silent in our prayer closets and our church altars, or should we cry to heaven until God moves on His throne and, as He has done many times in the past, stretches forth His hand and touches America again to renew and revive us? Ravenhill said, "The believers must make a last-ditch stand against this lax, loose, licentious, lustful age; for all that is lewd, crude, nude, and rude is a way of life. *If* the 'church' has anything to say, she had better wake up, stand up, speak up, or shut up. I hear faintly amidst this moral turpitude and tiredness a faint cry, 'Is there any word from the Lord?'"[12]

America in End-Time Prophecy

Irvin Baxter, Jr., has done much study on how America fits into biblical prophecy and the End Times. Baxter, along with many others, raises the question of why America is not clearly identified in the world government structure in the last days.

In the introduction, I referred the reader to Daniel's vision of the four beasts, recorded in Daniel 7. I also quoted some noted prophecy ministers who raise the question of why America cannot be positively identified in end-time prophecies. Some ministers identify the four beasts as England (lion), Germany (leopard), Russia (bear), and the World Kingdom of the Antichrist. However, the lion has eagles' wings, which many symbolize America since the eagle is the symbol of this nation. Furthermore, the eagles' wings grow from the body of the lion, just as the American colonies came from the nation of England. John the Revelator saw the fourth beast rising out of the sea, and he embodied the descriptions of the four beasts that Daniel saw in his vision.

> Then I stood on the sand of the sea. And I saw a beast rising up out of the sea, having seven heads and ten horns, and on his horns ten crowns, and on his heads a blasphemous name. Now the beast which I saw was like a leopard, his feet were like the feet of a bear, and his mouth like the mouth of a lion. The dragon gave him his power, his throne, and great authority.
>
> —Revelation 13:1–2

In Daniel 7, the eagle's wings (America) are present; but in Revelation 13, the eagle's wings are missing from the list of animals/symbols of the world powers. When the federated European government comes to power and receives its authority and power from the antichrist, where is America? It is the overwhelming opinion of prophecy scholars that the ten horns of Revelation refer to the European Federation led by the Antichrist.

There are various thoughts as to the reason for the absence of the eagles' wings in Revelation 13 and why America cannot be identified in other end-time prophecies. Some take the position that, should America continue in the direction she is headed, she will be absorbed by the European Federation led by the Antichrist, and will subsequently lose her identity as a world power.

Others believe that America will experience a great revival. They say that America will return to God, refuse to be part of the Federation, and will provide Israel a refuge and sanctuary when the Antichrist and his forces try to destroy Israel. The Bible says God will give Israel eagle's wings to fly to a haven or place of protection after two-thirds of Israel is destroyed. (Part of God's judgment upon Israel is allowing the Antichrist to destroy two-thirds of the population.)

> "And it shall come to pass in all the land," Says the LORD, "That two-thirds in it shall be cut off and die, But one-third shall be left in it."
>
> —ZECHARIAH 13:8

It is believed that the eagles' wings in Revelation 12:14 refer to America and her role in protecting Israel.

> But the woman was given two wings of a great eagle, that she might fly into the wilderness to her place, where she is nourished for a time and times and half a time, from the presence of the serpent.
>
> —REVELATION 12:14

Though America has pressured Israel to relinquish land for peace and has aligned herself with the United Nations regarding this issue, it is not outside the realm of reason that, should America experience a revival and turn again to God, God would again be America's divine protector and would use America to protect the remnant of Israel. This gives us hope that, in spite of everything happening that would cause God's judgment to fall, America could again enjoy God's favor. Should America follow the example of Nineveh and repent, God would pour out His Spirit upon this nation. America could indeed be a haven for Israel.

One thing is certain: America must have revival. If the people of God will unite in prayer and seek His face, then we will experience renewal and the blessings of God again. We can be a powerful force in turning America back to God.

Chapter 13
AWAKE, AMERICA!

God grants liberty only to those
who love it, and are always ready
to guard and defend it.[1]
—Daniel Webster

EARLIER IN THIS BOOK I DESCRIBED A VISION I had of a football field with several opposing teams squared off, each pair ignoring both the other teams on the field and the spectators in the stands. Those people in the stands weren't really spectators at all. Rather, they were engaged in all sorts of evil activities, paying no attention to the teams on the field. God showed me that the teams represented the various church denominations and churches, and the people in the stands stood for all the lost in the world. Just as the teams and spectators seemed absorbed in their own activities, oblivious to each other, the world looks elsewhere while churches clash with one another instead of helping people or intervening in their sinful actions.

Obviously, this is not the way it should be. This was not the intention of Christ in setting up His church. He did not shed His blood for the redemption of sins to watch His body ignore those He came to save. America needs a revival that is so powerful that the fire will burn down the walls that separate and divide the people of God; a revival so potent that churches will join hands in this war against Satan and secular humanism; a revival so pervasive that, once again, America will be known as a Christian nation with prayer and the Bible returned to our schools and government buildings; a revival so sweeping that from the Pacific to the Atlantic, from the Canadian border to the Mexican border, from Hawaii to Maine, and from Alaska to Florida, America will again learn to trust in our "superintending Providence;" a revival so awakening that Americans will rejoice, knowing that God has, indeed, "shed His grace on thee."

Reverend Carl Richardson told the following story:

> Shortly after the Civil War in America, the pleasure boat Robert E. Lee steamed out of Vicksburg, and headed down the mighty Mississippi River toward New Orleans. Hundreds of people were aboard. As scores of their loved ones waved to them on shore as it pushed off, little did they realize that this would be the final trip the Robert E. Lee would ever make.
>
> Sometime after midnight, it was discovered that the boat was on fire and the captain's first mate rushed down every corridor and passageway banging hurriedly on every door and shouting his warning, "Wake up! The boat's on fire!"
>
> He didn't have time to make any explanations. Too many lives were at stake for him to tarry for even a single moment. His duty was to knock on every door possible and deliver one warning, "Wake up! The boat's on fire!"
>
> As strange as it may seem, some people became angry at having been awakened so abruptly.... While some were angry, still others

were amused at the awakening. They thought it was a practical joke and were actually heard laughing for a few moments before the fiery holocaust entombed them.

Others heard the warning but just couldn't believe it and waited to hear it again more clearly.... And still others seemed never to have heard a single word of the warning. They were not the least bit conscious of any imminent danger, but slept on to the very moment of sudden death, and opened their eyes in another world.

But there were some who heard the warning and believed it to be true. They awakened from their sleep and made their escape to safety.

This is exactly the way the world treats the warnings from the Word of God.

But the boat's on fire! Jesus Christ is coming again soon! Judgment is ahead!

Either the minister/watchman will run the corridors and bang on the doors and cry "Wake up! The ship is on fire," or they will allow the masses to continue to be lulled asleep and perish in the flames.

The boat is on fire! America is at peril. Someone needs to sound the alarm and rally the troops, the Body of Christ, and wake up America and bring revival once again across this country. I hope you, reader, are among those who have read and understood this message and are among those to whom it will be said at the end of the way:

When the question sounded, "Watchman what of the night?" you sounded the alarm. Because of your diligence, your alertness, your action, your faith, your prayers, your support of the Body, and your efforts; America will once again turn to God and experience renewal and revival.[2]

The Unity of the Body

> And the LORD said, "Indeed the people are one and they all have one language, and this is what they begin to do; now nothing that they propose to do will be withheld from them.
>
> —GENESIS 11:6

> When the Day of Pentecost had fully come, they were all with one accord in one place.
>
> —ACTS 2:1

God poured out His Spirit upon a group of people that were *together*. They were in one accord, a great revival broke out, and three thousand souls were added to their number.

> Now the multitude of those who believed were of one heart and one soul; neither did anyone say that any of the things he possessed was his own, but they had all things in common. And with great power the apostles gave witness.
>
> —ACTS 4:32–33

When people are of one heart and one soul, they will experience great power to do the will and work of God.

> But when they did not find them, they dragged Jason and some brethren to the rulers of the city, crying out, "These who have turned the world upside down have come here too."
>
> —Acts 17:6

When the people of God are together, they can turn the world upside down. We might think we are outmanned and underpowered, but that is not the case. When the shepherd Moses walked down the corridor of the great Egyptian palace, he—not Pharaoh—was in control. God has called us to deliver His people from the bondage of Egypt and the tyranny of the pharaohs of this world: "You are of God, little children, and have overcome them, because He who is in you is greater than he who is in the world" (1 John 4:4).

The body of Christ has lost much freedom in America. Some Christians have also lost their joy, their power, their direction, their vision, their desire, and their hunger for revival. When King David and his men returned to Ziklag, they discovered the Amalekites had kidnapped their families, stolen their possessions, destroyed their homes, and burned their city. They cried unto the Lord, and David inquired, "Shall I pursue this troop?" God answered, "Pursue, for you shall surely overtake them and without fail recover all" (1 Sam. 30:8). God told David not to leave his family and possessions in the hands of the enemy. David had lost it, but, through God, he would get it all back.

This lesson is important to the body of Christ in America. Yes, the Supreme Court and political leaders have robbed us of freedom, and they are trying to rob us of our children and our possessions. But our commander-in-chief is God.

He is telling every blood-bought Christian to go forward and "without fail recover all."

The greatest tragedy of the body of Christ is that churches fail to fight the devil and his demons because they are too busy fighting one another. What does the world see when they look at Christianity? Ministers who debate and compete with one another. Churches that have borrowed their advertising slogans from the secular world and use the same sales pitch as the car salesman on television.

Many Christians pattern themselves after the political parties. They seem to have more loyalty to the party than to the country. Many churches are the same way; they have a greater loyalty to their denomination than to the kingdom of God.

I was having breakfast in a restaurant when a young man approached me and asked if I were a minister. When I told him I was, he introduced himself as the youth pastor of the largest church in that area. When I told him I would like to have lunch with him some day, he asked what church I attended. When I told him, he said he could not have lunch with me because we were too far apart doctrinally. I asked him if he were a born-again Christian. He replied that he was, and I told him that I was also a born again believer, which made us brothers. I said that he might not want me for a brother, but there wasn't anything he could do about it because the blood of Jesus made us that way.

Though I remember facing religious discrimination and persecution in my youth, I thought that the body of Christ had in large part gotten past race, gender, and religious prejudices. I believed that we were moving to the place where we could all concentrate on the things that are important to the God who saved and called us into this marvelous ministry.

Sadly, there is more work to do in these areas in order to live out Jesus' command to love.

> A new commandment I give to you, that you love one another; as I have loved you, that you also love one another. By this all will know that you are My disciples, if you have love for one another.
>
> —JOHN 13:34–35

Why are Christians always searching for the areas of disagreement between denominations and groups, rather than the areas of agreement? There are only two questions that we should really be interested in to determine if we can work together: Do you believe that Jesus Christ is the Son of God? Have you accepted Christ as your personal Savior and Lord of your life, along with the provisions of His grace, which would make you a born-again believer? We can disagree on a hundred other things, but none of them are life-and-death matters. Why do we break fellowship over different views of Scripture when we are born again believers? When I meet a Christian, I try to find out what we have in common. I look for common ground. I look for something that will bind us together.

Paul wrote the following about the unity of the body of Christ:

> So we, being many, are one body in Christ, and individually members of one another.... Be kindly

> affectionate to one another with brotherly love, in honor giving preference to one another.
>
> —Romans 12:5, 10

> For as the body is one and has many members, but all the members of that one body, being many, are one body, so also is Christ. For by one Spirit we were all baptized into one body—whether Jews or Greeks, whether slaves or free—and have all been made to drink into one Spirit. For in fact the body is not one member but many.
>
> —1 Corinthians 12:12–14

> Therefore, as we have opportunity, let us do good to all, especially to those who are of the household of faith.
>
> —Galatians 6:10

These Scriptures are as true today as they were at any time in history. The Word says, "Blessed is the nation whose God is the Lord" (Ps. 33:12). Let's focus on making Him our Lord rather than on minor doctrinal differences that have no bearing on our salvation.

My prayer is that God will use someone to rally all born-again believers in America and marshal a mighty prayer force that will join hearts, hands, and voices together. May the echo not only reverberate throughout America, but around the world. Now is not the time to become defensive or to retreat. We need to go into the enemy's camp and tear down the strongholds of Satan and wake up America.

Appendix A
THE PLAN

OVER FIVE YEARS AGO, THE LORD SHARED WITH me a plan of renewal for America, which I call Awake, America. Awake, America is merely about cooperation across denominational lines in an effort to bring prayer, the Word of God, revival, and renewal back to the church and society in America. The plan begins with a simple recognition that we are brothers and sisters in Christ and that we must work together to fulfill the Great Commission.

> And Jesus came and spoke to them, saying, "All authority has been given to Me in heaven and on earth. Go therefore and make disciples of all the nations, baptizing them in the name of the Father and of the Son and of the Holy Spirit, teaching them to observe all things that I have commanded you; and lo, I am with you always, even to the end of the age."
>
> —MATTHEW 28:18–19

> You are of God, little children, and have overcome them, because He who is in you is greater than he who is in the world.... Beloved, let us love one another, for love is of God; and everyone who loves is born of God and knows God.
>
> —1 JOHN 4:4, 7

I fervently believe that God wants us to unite in our efforts and our prayers until America is shaken by His power!

Awake, America is not a new organization or structure that will take the place of any existing bodies or groups. Instead, it will highlight what the existing groups are doing and will provide a forum for all of these various groups to cooperate in order to make a greater impact on America. The voices of the Christian body must be one voice.

The foundation of Awake, America's strategy is prayer. Our first priority is to involve the entire body of Christ—every denomination, organization, fellowship, television network, magazine, local congregation, and individual—in a cooperative effort to implement a plan of consistent intercessory prayer.

If you have a heart for unity within the body of Christ and a vision for renewal, I pray that you would contact me or visit the Awake, America Web site to find out more information about how to implement this plan in your community. The future of our children and our grandchildren and the spiritual health of our churches depend upon your help.

www.awakeamerica.us

Then conquer we must
When our cause it is just,
And this be our motto:
"In God is our Trust"
And the star-spangled banner
In triumph shall wave,
O'er the land of the free
And the home of the brave.

—"The Star-Spangled Banner"
by FRANCIS SCOTT KEY

INDEX

V

W

NOTES

Abraham Lincoln Proclamation

1. Abraham Lincoln, "Proclamation Appointing a National Fast Day, March 30, 1863," *The Collected Works of Abraham Lincoln,* Vol. 6, ed. Roy P. Basler (New Brunswick, NJ: Rutgers University Press, 1953), 157.

Dedication

1. William Wirt Henry, ed., *Patrick Henry: Life, Correspondence and Speeches,* Vol. I (New York: Charles Scribner's Sons, 1891), 266.

Introduction

1. Scott S. Dowlen, "Does the Bible Tell the Future?" http://bible.dowlen.net/content.php?article.2 (accessed January 20, 2008).

2. Ibid.

3. Irving Baxter, Jr., "The Prophetic Future of the United States," *Endtime Magazine* (November–December 2000): 30.

4. Benjamin Franklin, "For Prayers in the Convention," *The Writings of Benjamin Franklin: Collected and Edited with a Life and Introduction,* Volume IX: 1783-1788, ed. Albert Henry Smyth (New York: The Macmillan Company, 1906), 601.

5. "[Lest] there be any fornicator or profane person like Esau, who for one morsel of food sold his birthright. For you know that afterward, when he wanted to inherit the blessing, he was rejected, for he found no place for repentance, though he sought it diligently with tears" (Heb. 12:16–17). (See also Genesis 25:29–34.)

6. Leonard Ravenhill, *America Is Too Young to Die* (Pensacola, FL: Christian Life Books, 2005), 99.

7. Ibid., 102.

8. William J. Federer, *The Interesting History of Income Tax* (St. Louis, MO: AmeriSearch, 2004), 69.

9. Ibid.

10. Ronald Reagan, "Speech Announcing Presidential Candidacy," *Tear Down this Wall: the Reagan Revolution—A National Review History* (New York: Continuum, 2004), 16–17.

Chapter 1: A Nation Under Siege

1. Michael Martin and Leonard Gelber, *Dictionary of American History* (Totowa, NJ: Roman & Littlefield, 1978), 166.

2. For a collection of writings on pre-9/11 American attitudes toward the use of the military, as well as about U.S. defense in general, see *American Defense Policy*, 7th edition, ed. Peter L. Hays, Brenda J. Vallance, and Alan R. Van Tassel (Baltimore, MD: Johns Hopkins University Press, 1997).

3. Chief Architect Minoru Yamasaki made this interesting comment: "The World Trade Center is a living symbol of man's dedication to world peace... [It] should... become a representation of man's belief in humanity, his need for individual dignity, his beliefs in the cooperation of men, and... his ability to find greatness." "World Trade Center," *The Great Buildings Collection*, http://www.greatbuildings.com/buildings/World_Trade_Center.html (accessed January 22, 2008).

4. Jeff Kunerth, "Iraq's Rich History Alludes to Potential as Great Nation," *Orlando Sentinel*, http://www.freerepublic.com/focus/fr/815231/posts (accessed January 20, 2008).

5. J. N. Postgate, *Early Mesopotamia: Society and Economy at the Dawn of History* (London and New York: Routledge, 1994), xxi.

6. "Great Wall of China at Bejing," http://www.chinapage.com/friend/goh/beijing/greatwall/greatwall.html (accessed March 5, 2008).

7. Edward Gibbon, *The History of the Decline and Fall of the Roman Empire,* Vol. IV (New York: Harper & Brothers, 1880), 90.

8. Fred C. Schwarz, *You Can Trust the Communists (to Be Communists),* Christian Anti-Communism Campaign (2000) http://www.schwarzreport.org/ (accessed February 25, 2008).

9. Neville Chamberlain, *Speeches that Changed the World* (London: Quercus, 2006), 77.

10. Winston Churchill, "Blood, Toil, Tears and Sweat," *Never Give In! The Best of Winston Churchill's Speeches*, ed. Winston S. Churchill (New York: Hyperion, 2003), 204.

11. Ibid., "Wars Are Not Won by Evacuations," 218.

12. Ibid., "This Was Their Finest Hour," 229.

Chapter 2: A Foundation to Freedom

1. Federer, *Treasury of Presidential Quotations* (St. Louis, MO: AmeriSearch, 2004), 201.

2. Ace Collins, *Songs Sung Red, White, and Blue: The Stories Behind America's Best-loved Patriotic Songs* (New York: HarperSources, 2003), 15–16.

3. "The Declaration of Independence," *The National Archives*, http://www.archives.gov/exhibits/charters/declaration_transcript.html (accessed February 25, 2008).

4. Alexis de Tocqueville, *Democracy in America*, trans. Henry Reeve and Francis Bowen (Wordsworth Editions, 1998), 120.

5. Larry Pahl, *The Late, Great USA: What the Bible Says about the Coming Iraqi War* (InstantPublisher.com, 2003).

6. "The Act of Supremacy, 1534," *English History in the Making*, Vol. I, ed. William L. Sachse (New York: John Wiley and Sons, 1967), 187–188.

7. Brian R. Farmer, *American Conservatism: History, Theory, and Practice* (Newcastle, UK: Cambridge Scholars Press, 2005), 103.

8. Charles Reagan Wilson, "Religion and the American Civil War in Comparative Perspective," *Religion and the American Civil War*, (New York: Oxford University Press, 1998), 386.

9. Kevin P. Phillips, *The Cousins' War: Religion, Politics, & the Triumph of Anglo-America* (New York: Basic Books, 2000), 60.

10. "The Charters of Freedom," *The National Archives*, http://www.archives.gov/national-archives-experience/charters/bill_of_rights.html (accessed January 25, 2008).

11. Bernard H. Siegan, *The Supreme Court's Constitution: An Inquiry into Judicial Review and Its Impact on Society* (New Brunswick, NJ: Transaction Books, 1987), 114.

12. It is often mentioned that Thomas Jefferson used the phrase "wall of separation between church and State." Jefferson was not himself a member of the Congress that wrote the Amendment. His actions as president also belie a strict separation of church and State. (See Siegan, *The Supreme Court's Constitution*, 120.)

13. See Siegan, *The Supreme Court's Constitution,* 121. "Even here, the framers were concerned with federal government, not states. Madison and the House sought to restrict states' power only over free exercise and not over establishment."

14. *Engle v. Vitale*, 370 U.S. 421 (1962).

15. David Limbaugh, *Persecution: How Liberals are Waging War*

Against Christians (Washington, DC: Regnery Publishing, 2003), 19.
16. *Engle v. Vitale*, 370 U.S. 421 (1962).
17. Ibid.
18. George Goldberg, *Church, State and the Constitution: The Religion Clauses Upside Down* (Washington, DC: Regnery Gateway, 1987), 69–70.
19. Limbaugh, *Persecution*, 20.
20. Ibid.
21. Siegan, *The Supreme Court's Constitution*, 21.
22. Thomas Paine, *Common Sense*, accessed on Archiving Early America site, http://www.earlyamerica.com/earlyamerica/milestones/commonsense/text.html (accessed January 25, 2008).
23. Ibid.
24. Collins, *Songs Sung Red, White, and Blue*, 15–16.

Chapter 3: God's Favor Upon America

1. "Jamestown Church," *Jamestown Rediscovery*, http://www.apva.org/tour/chtour.html (accessed January 26, 2008).
2. Sydney E. Alhstrom, *A Religious History of the American People*, 2nd ed. (New Haven, CT: Yale University Press, 2004), 187.
3. Federer, *America's God and Country: Encyclopedia of Quotations* (Coppell, TX: Fame Publishing, 1996), 456–457.
4. Benjamin Rush, *Essays: Literary, Moral and Philosophical*, 2nd ed. (Philadelphia: Thomas and William Bradford, 1806), 8.
5. Federer, *America's God and Country: Encyclopedia of Quotations*, 8.
6. Jared Sparks, ed., *The Writings of George Washington: Being His Correspondence, Addresses, Messages, and Other Papers, Official and Private,* Vol. XII (Boston: American Stationers' Company, John B. Russell, 1837), 167.
7. Seth Ames, ed., *Works of Fisher Ames with a Selection from His Speeches and Correspondence* (Boston: Little, Brown and Company, 1854), 82.
8. Albert Ellery Bergh, ed., *The Writings of Thomas Jefferson,* Vol. IX (Washington, DC: The Thomas Jefferson Memorial Association), 376–377.
9. Charles R. King, ed., *The Life and Correspondence of Rufus King: Comprising His Letters, Private and Official, His Public Documents and His Speeches,* Vol. VI (New York: G. P. Putnam's Sons, 1900), 276.

10. Ibid., 276.

11. Samuel Adams, "An Oration Delivered at the State-House," *The Life and Public Services of Samuel Adams,* Vol. III, ed. William V. Wells (Boston: Little, Brown, and Company, 1865), 408.

12. Stanley L. Klos, *President Who? Forgotten Founders* (Carnegie, PA: Estoric.com, 2004), http://www.johnhancock.org (accessed January 20, 2008).

13. Charles Francis Adams, *Familiar Letters of John Adams and His Wife Abigail Adams, During the Revolution* (New York: Hurd and Houghton, 1876), 188.

14. "Orderly Book, 9 July, 1776," in *The Writings of George Washington,* ed. Worthington Chauncey Ford (New York & London: G. P. Putnam's Sons, 1889), 223.

15. Daniel L. Dreisbach, Mark D. Hall, and Jeffry H. Morrison, eds., *The Founders on God and Government* (Lanham, MD: Rowman & Littlefield Publishers, 2004), 7.

16. William J. Johnson, *George Washington, the Christian* (New York: The Abingdon Press, 1919), 26–27.

17. John Adams, "To the Officers of the First Brigade of the Third Division of the Militia of Massachusetts, 11 October, 1798," *The Works of John Adams, Second President of the United States: with A Life of the Author, Notes and Illustrations,* Vol. IX, ed. Charles Francis Adams (Boston: Little, Brown and Company, 1854), 229.

18. Andrew A. Lipscomb and Albert Ellery Bergh, eds., T*he Writings of Thomas Jefferson,* Vol. XIII (Washington, DC: The Thomas Jefferson Memorial Association, 1905), 385. (The published writings of Jefferson document only the first of these two sentences in a letter to Charles Thompson dated January 9, 1816.)

19. John Jay, "To John Murray, Jun," *The Life of John Jay with Selections from His Correspondence and Miscellaneous Papers,* Vol. II, ed. William Jay (New York: J. & J. Harper, 1833), 376.

20. Federer, *America's God and Country,* 206.

21. Ellis Sandoz, *A Government of Laws: Political Theory, Religion, and the American Founding* (Columbia, MO: University of Missouri Press, 2001), 141.

22. Charles W. Eliot, ed., *American Historical Documents, 1000–1904* (New York: P F Collier & Son, 1910), 63.

23. William MacDonald, ed., *Select Charters and Other Documents Illustrative of American History 1606–1775* (New York: The Macmillan Company, 1899), 94.

24. B. F. Morris, ed., *Christian Life and Character of the Civil Institutions of the United States, Developed in the Official and Historical Annals of the Republic* (Philadelphia: George W. Childs, 1864), 88.

25. David W. Hall, ed., T*he Genevan Reformation and the American Founding*, (Lanham, MD: Lexington Books, 2003), 320.

26. MacDonald, ed., *Pennsylvania Charter of Privileges, in Select Charters and Other Documents Illustrative of American History 1606–1775*, 225.

27. "The Charters of Freedom."

28. William Jennings Bryan and Francis W. Halsey, eds., *The World's Famous Orations, Vol. VIII* (New York and London: Funk and Wagnalls, 1906), 65–67.

29. Henry, ed., *Patrick Henry: Life, Correspondence and Speeches,* Vol. II, 592.

30. Federer, *America's God and Country*, 289.

31. "Acts of Congress in Regard to the Bible," *Papers of the American Historical Association,* Vol. II (New York & London: G. P. Putnam's Sons, 1888), 125–126. Note that while the vote was in favor of the purchase, the action was not executed. However, in 1781Congress "passed a resolution approving" a report favorable toward and recommending to U.S. citizens a Bible published by Robert Aitken. (See Henry Barker, *English Bible Versions* [New York: Edwin S. Gorham, 1907], 255.)

32. David K. Watson, *History of American Coinage* (New York and London: G. P. Putnam's Sons, 1899), 214.

33. Ibid., 212.

34. Diane Ravitch, ed., *The American Reader: Words that Moved a Nation,* 2nd Edition (New York: Perennial, 2000), 315. In Newdow v. U.S. Congress (2002), the Ninth Circuit Court of Appeals declared the Pledge of Allegiance unconstitutional because of the words *under God.* (See Edward R. Sharkey, Jr., and Kendra B. Stewart, "Terrorism, Security, and Civil Liberties: The State Responds," *American National Security and Civil Liberties in an Era of Terrorism*, ed. David B. Cohen and John W. Wells [New York: Palgrave Macmillan, 2004], 142.)

35. "Educational Resources," The American Flag Foundation, Inc., http://www.americanflagfoundation.org/content/educationalresources_pledgestory.cfm (accessed January 21, 2008).

36. Melani McAlister, *Epic Encounters: Culture, Media, and U.S.*

Interests in the Middle East, 1945–2000 (Berkeley: University of California Press, 2001), 33.

37. Michael McGarry, "Israel: Christian View," *A Dictionary of the Jewish-Christian Dialogue, Expanded Edition, ed. Leon Klenicki and Geoffrey Wigoder* (New York: Paulist Press, 1995), 103–104.

38. Paul Charles Merkley, *Christian Attitudes Toward the State of Israel* (Montreal and Ithaca, New York: McGill-Queen's University Press, 2001), 167.

39. Ibid., 167–168.

40. Franklin, "For Prayers in the Convention," 600–601.

41. Federer, *America's God and Country*, 399.

42. Bob Kelly, *Worth Repeating: More than 5,000 Classic and Contemporary Quotes* (Grand Rapids, MI: Kregel Academic & Professional, 2003), 28.

43. Charles Gaines, *Perspective* (Fairfax, Virginia: Xulon Press, 2006), 97.

44. Howard W. Duffield, "The Lineage of an American Patriot," *The Magazine of History with Notes and Queries* (November–December 1916): 222.

45. Gaines, *Perspective*, 98.

46. Ibid.

47. Ulysses S. Grant, "To Sunday-School Children in S. S. Times," *A Personal History of Ulysses S. Grant*, ed. Albert D. Richardson (Whitefish, MT: Kessinger Publishing, 2006), 630.

48. Federer, *Treasury of Presidential Quotations*, 177.

49. Federer, *America's God and Country*, 296.

50. Harry S. Truman, "Address Before the Attorney General's Conference on Law Enforcement Problems," http://www.presidency.ucsb.edu/ws/index.php?pid=13707&st=&st1= (accessed January 20, 2008). Also quoted in Federer, *Treasury of Presidential Quotations*, 292.

51. Federer, *America's God and Country*, 697.

52. Noah Webster, *History of the United States* (New Haven, CT: Durrie & Peck; Louisville, KY: Wilcox, Dickerman, & Co., 1832), 1.

53. Federer, *America's God and Country*, 181.

54. Donald S. Lutz and Charles S. Hyneman, "The Relative Influence of European Writers on Late Eighteenth-Century American Political Thought," *The American Political Science Review* (March 1984): 189–197.

55. Gaines, *Perspective*, 98.

56. Charles Willis Pickering, *Supreme Chaos: The Politics of Judicial Confirmation & the Culture War* (Macon, GA: Stroud and Hall, 2005), 50–51.

57. House proceedings for January 23, 2008, notes that prayer was offered by the Reverend Saúl Santos, Jr., at 10:04 a.m., http://clerk.house.gov/floorsummary/floor.html (accessed January 27, 2008).

58. Franklin, "For Prayers in the Convention," 601.

59. George Washington, "First Inaugural Address, 1789," *United States House of Representatives*, http://www.house.gov/forbes/prayer/prayerincongress.htm (accessed January 27, 2008).

60. Peter Marshall, *The United States House of Representatives* http://www.house.gov/forbes/prayer/prayerincongress.htm (accessed January 27, 2008).

61. John Quincy Adams, "An Oration Delivered Before the Inhabitants of the Town of Newburyport, at Their Request, on the Sixty-First Anniversary of the Declaration of Independence, July 4, 1837" (Newburyport, MA: Charles Whipple, 1837), 5–6.

62. Michael Burlington and Noah Brooks, eds., *Lincoln Observed: The Civil War Dispatches of Noah Brooks* (Baltimore: John Hopkins Press, 1998).

63. "Breakfast in Washington," *Time* (15 February, 1954).

64. Ronald Reagan, *State of the Union Addresses* (Whitefish, MT: Kessinger, 2004), 37.

65. Peter Schweizer, *Victory: The Reagan Administration's Secret Strategy that Hastened the Collapse of the Soviet Union* (New York: Atlantic Monthly Press, 1996).

66. Paul Kengor, *God and Ronald Reagan: A Spiritual Life* (New York: ReganBooks, 2004), 325.

67. Samuel Adams, "To James Warren," *The Writings of Samuel Adams*, ed. Harry Alonzo Cushing (New York: G. P. Putnam's Sons, 1908), 124.

68. Federer, *Backfired: A Nation Born for Religious Tolerance No Longer Tolerates Religion* (St. Louis, MO: AmeriSearch, 2005), 198.

69. Gouverneur Morris, "Notes on the Form of a Constitution for France," *The Life of Gouverneur Morris: With Selections from His Correspondence and Miscellaneous Papers,* Vol. III, ed. Jared Sparks (Boston: Gray & Bowen, 1832), 483.

70. Franklin Pearce, "Inaugural Address," *A Compilation of the Messages and Papers of the Presidents 1789-1897, Vol. 5*, ed. James D. Richardson (Washington, DC: Government Printing Office, 1897),

203.

71. Rutherford B. Hayes, "Inaugural Address," *Letters and Messages of Rutherford B. Hayes, President of the United States* (Washington, DC, 1881), 16.

Chapter 4: A Nation at Risk

1. Daniel Webster, *The Works of Daniel Webster,* Vol. 1, ed. Edward Everett (Boston: Charles C. Little and James Brown, 1851), 403–404.

2. Millard F. Caldwell, "Cicero's Prognosis," Presented at the 22nd Annual Meeting of the Association of American Physicians and Surgeons, Inc., October 7–9, 1965, reprinted March 1996, American Family Association of Mississippi, http://www.afams.net/cicero.htm.

3. Lipscomb and Bergh, eds., *The Writings of Thomas Jefferson,* Vol. II (Washington, DC: The Thomas Jefferson Memorial Association, 1904), 225.

4. *Whitney v. California*, 274 U.S. 357 (1927).

5. Abraham Lincoln, "Gettysburg Address," *Abraham Lincoln: His Speeches and Writings*, ed. Roy P. Basler (New York: Da Capo Press, 2001), 737.

6. Daniel Webster, "Second Speech on Foot's Resolution," *The Works of Daniel Webster,* Vol. III, ed. Edward Everett (Boston: Charles C. Little and James Brown, 1851), 321.

7. Matthew J. Streb, "The Reemergence of the Academic Freedom Debate," *Academic Freedom at the Dawn of a New Century*, eds. Evan Gerstmann and Matthew J. Streb (Stanford, CA: Stanford University Press, 2006), 16.

8. W. Somerset Maugham, *Strictly Personal* (New York: Doubleday, 1941), 216.

9. Mark Wilensky, *The Elementary Common Sense of Thomas Paine* (Arvada, CO: 13 Stars Publishing, 2005), 55.

10. Paul Leicester Ford, ed., *The Writings of Thomas Jefferson,* Vol. IV (New York and London: G. P. Putnam's Sons, 1894), 467.

11. John Adams, "Letters to John Taylor, of Caroline, Virginia, in Reply to His Strictures on Some Parts of the Defence of the American Constitutions," *Works of John Adams, Second President of the United States: with A Life of the Author, Notes and Illustrations,* Vol. VI, ed. Charles Francis Adams (Boston: Little, Brown and Company, 1851), 484.

12. "The Flag Raisers," *Iwo Jima, Inc.*, http://www.iwojima.com/

(accessed January 27, 2008). Also, see James Bradley, *Flags of Our Fathers* (New York: Bantam Books, 2006).

13. "U.S.M.C. War Memorial," *U.S. National Park Service*, http://www.nps.gov/archive/gwmp/usmc.htm (accessed January 2, 2008).

14. Tom Brokaw, *The Greatest Generation* (New York: Random House, 1998).

15. Federer, *America's God and Country*, 20.

16. Percival Everett, ed., "Introduction," *The Jefferson Bible* (New York: Akashic Books, 2004), 12.

17. John Cook, *The Book of Positive Quotations,* 2nd Ed., ed. Steve Deger and Leslie Ann Gibson (Minneapolis: Fairview Press, 2007), 507.

18. Captain Stephen R. Ellison's story is used by permission. http://www.kilroywashere.org/007-Pages/07-Letters.html (accessed January 16, 2008). Dr. Ellison himself served with distinction and in areas where he was at great risk.

19. "High School Survey Generates National Response," John S. and James L. Knight Foundation (Spring 2005), http://www.knightfdn.org/default_print.asp?story=news_at_knight/newsletters/64_spring2005/05_jou-briefs.html (accessed December 2007).

20. "U. S. religious landscape in flux," *MSNBC.com* (February 25, 2008), http://www.msnbc.msn.com/id/23337807/ (accessed April 4, 2008).

21. Elmer Davis, *By Elmer Davis*, ed. Robert Lloyd Davis (Indianapolis, IN: Bobbs-Merrill, 1964), 90.

22. The religious make-up of the Founding Fathers, including signers of the Declaration of Independence, can be found at http://www.adherents.com/gov/Founding_Fathers_Religion.html (accessed January 27, 2008).

23. Steven Fantina, *Of Thee I Speak: A Collection of Patriotic Quotes, Essays, and Speeches* (Phillipsburg, NJ: Integritous Press, 2006), 3.

24. Franklin, "For Prayers in the Convention," 601.

25. Douglas Brinkley, "Remembering Reagan," *U.S. News & World Report*, May 29, 2005, http://www.usnews.com/usnews/news/articles/050606/6reagan.htm (accessed April 4, 2008). The original article by Lance Morrow may be found at "June 6, 1944," *Time*, May 28, 1984, http://www.time.com/time/magazine/article/0,9171,951085,00.html (accessed April 4, 2008).

Chapter 5: Secular Humanism

1. Steve Bruce, "Revelations: The Future of the New Christian Right," *Fundamentalism in Comparative Perspective*, ed. Lawrence Kaplan (Amherst: University of Massachusetts Press, 1992), 62.

2. "What is Secular Humanism?" *Christian Answers Network*, http://www.christiananswers.net/q-sum/sum-r002.html (accessed January 29, 2008).

3. Council for Secular Humanism, http://www.secularhumanism.org/ (accessed January 29, 2008).

4. Jim Walsh, Frank Kemerer, and Laurie Maniotis, *The Educator's Guide to Texas School Law, 6th Ed.* (Austin: University of Texas Press, 2005), 271. Note that in *Smith v. Board of School Commissioners of Mobile County* (1987), the judge *did* decide that "secular humanism constituted a religion for establishment clause purposes" (272), but the decision was reversed by a higher court.

5. Limbaugh, *Persecution*, 65.

6. "Humanist Manifesto I," *American Humanist Association*, http://www.americanhumanist.org/about/manifesto1.html (accessed January 29, 2008).

7. "Humanist Manifesto III," *American Humanist Association*, http://www.americanhumanist.org/3/HumandItsAspirations.htm (accessed January 29, 2008).

8. "Ten Commandments Monument Moved," CNN.com, November 14, 2003, http://www.cnn.com/2003/LAW/08/27/ten.commandments (accessed January 16, 2008).

9. *Abington Township School District v. Schempp*, 374 U.S. 203 (1963).

10. Newt Gingrich, *Winning the Future: A 21st Century Contract with America* (Washington, DC: Regnery, 2005), 68.

11. "Ten Commandments Monument Moved," CNN.com.

12. Bergh, ed. T*he Writings of Thomas Jefferson,* Vol. XVII (Washington, DC: The Thomas Jefferson Memorial Association, 1907), 381. The full quote, in Jefferson's *Kentucky Resolutions*, is, "…no power over the freedom of religion, freedom of speech, or freedom of the press being delegated to the United States by the Constitution, nor prohibited by it to the States, all lawful powers respecting the same did of right remain, and were reserved to the States or the people."

13. *IAM v. Street*, 367 US 740 (1961).

14. Church Baldwin, "The American Inquisition Has Begun," November 15, 2003, http://www.chuckbaldwinlive.com/Ed_15Nov03

.html (accessed January 16, 2008).

15. "Facts on Induced Abortion in the United States," May 2006, Guttmacher Institute, http://www.guttmacher.org/ pubs/fb_induced_abortion.html#3 (accessed January 16, 2008).

16. Lawence B. Finer and Stanley K. Henshaw, "Estimates of U.S. Abortion Incidence, 2001–2003," August 3, 2006, Guttmacher Institute, http://www.guttmacher.org/pubs/2006/08/03/ab_incidence.pdf (accessed January 16, 2008).

17. Adam Schiff, "The Battle of America," September 14, 2001, http://schiff.house.gov/HoR/CA29/Newsroom/Op-Eds+-+Statements+and+Letters/The+Battle+of+America.htm (accessed January 17, 2008).

18. AFA Alert, March 2004, *American Family Association.*

19. Joyce Appleby and Terence Ball, eds., *Jefferson: Political Writings* (New York: Cambridge University Press, 1999), 80.

20. Ford, ed., *The Writings of Thomas Jefferson,* Vol. III (New York and London: G. P. Putnam's Sons, 1894), 267.

21. Henry S. Sussman, *High Resolution: Critical Theory and the Problem of Literacy* (New York: Oxford University Press, 1989), 7–8.

22. "Senate Passes Bill to Protect Gays from Hate Crimes," CBC News, April 28, 2004, http://www.cbc.ca/story/canada/national/2004/04/28/hatelaw040428.html (accessed January 28, 2008).

23. For additional information, see David F. Dawes, "Pro-gay Bill C-250 Will Now Become Law," CanadianChristianity.com, http://www.canadianchristianity.com/cgi-bin/na.cgi?nationalupdates/040428bill (accessed January 30, 2008). To place Bill C-250 within a larger context in Canada, see David F. Dawes, "Marriage Rocked by Politics, Protest and Prayer," CanadianChristianity.com, http://www.canadianchristianity.com/cgi-bin/na.cgi?nationalupdates/030918marriage (accessed January 28, 2008).

24. Lars Grip, "No Free Speech in Preaching," *Christianity Today,* August 9, 2004, http://www.christianitytoday.com/ct/2004/augustweb-only/8-9-12.0.html (accessed January 21, 2008).

25. Art Moore, "Evangelist's 'Tone Incited Hatred of Muslims,'" *WorldNetDaily*, November 5, 2003, http://www.worldnetdaily.com/news/article.asp?ARTICLE_ID=35432 (accessed January 16, 2008).

26. "Stifling Unpopular Speech: This Wasn't Supposed to Happen Here," *Issues & Views* March 14, 2005, http://www.issues-views.com/index.php/sect/21000/article/21098 (accessed January 31, 2008).

27. "The Affirmations of Humanism: A Statement of Principles."
28. Ibid.
29. Ibid.
30. Ibid.
31. Ibid.
32. Ibid.

Chapter 6: Activist Judges

1. "Quotes," *The Southern Messenger*, http://www.southernmessenger.org/historical_quotes.htm (accessed February 26, 2008).

2. *Kelo v. City of New London*, 545 U.S. 469 (2005).

3. *American Communications Association v. Douds*, 339 U.S. 382 (1950).

4. *Lawrence v. Texas*, 539 U.S. 558 (2003).

5. Thomas Abshier, "The Supreme Court and Religion," November 8, 1995, http://www.doctorsenator.com/SupremeCourtandReligion.html (accessed January 17, 2008).

6. Abshier, "The Supreme Court and Religion."

7. Lipscomb and Bergh, eds., *The Writings of Thomas Jefferson,* Vol. XI (Washington, DC: The Thomas Jefferson Memorial Association, 1904), 51.

8. Ibid., 277.

9. H. A. Washington, ed., *The Writings of Thomas Jefferson: Being His Autobiography, Correspondence, Reports, Messages, Addresses, and Other Writings, Official and Private,* Vol. VII (Washington, DC: Taylor & Maury, 1854), 322.

10. Abshier, "The Supreme Court and Religion."

11. William Bondy, *The Separation of Governmental Powers in History, in Theory, and in the Constitutions* (Clark, NJ: The Lawbook Exchange, 2004), 128.

12. Ibid.

13. Ibid, 129.

14. Abshier, "The Supreme Court and Religion."

15. Francis Newton Thorpe, ed., *The Statesmanship of Andrew Jackson as Told in His Writings and Speeches* (New York: The Tandy-Thomas Company, 1909), 164–165.

16. Abraham Lincoln, "First Inaugural Address, March 4, 1861," *The Collected Works of Abraham Lincoln,* Vol. 4, ed. Roy P. Basler (Rutgers, NJ: Rutgers University Press, 1953), 269.

17. Ibid.

18. Limbaugh, *Persecution*, 201.

19. Kevin A. Ring, ed., *Scalia Dissents: Writings of the Supreme Court's Wittiest, Most Outspoken Justice* (Washington, D.C.: Regnery, 2004), xi.

20. Pat Robertson, "Operation Supreme Court Freedom: A Letter from Pat Robertson," CBN, http://www.cbn.com/special/supremeCourt/prayerpledge.asp (accessed January 17, 2008).

21. Limbaugh, *Persecution*, 5. Limbaugh also notes that the judge "prohibited references to other deities" (5), but that "in reality [the Court's language] was targeted solely at Christian prayer, because it was the only kind at issue" (6).

22. "Judge: Legislative Prayers Can't Mention Jesus," WRTV, November 30, 2005, http://www.theindychannel.com/ news/5436497/detail.html (accessed January 20, 2008).

23. *Hinrichs v. Bosma*, 400 F. Supp. 2d 1103, 1105 (S.D. Ind. 2005) 59.

24. "Judge: Legislative Prayers Can't Mention Jesus."

25. Mike Lewis, "Court Answers House Prayer: Ruling Overturned that Prayer Violates Separation of Church and State," *Times–Mail,* October 31, 2007, <http://www.tmnews.com/stories/2007/10/31/news.nw-837547.tms (accessed January 20, 2008). In a ruling announced October 30, 2007, Hamilton's decision was overturned by the 7th U.S. Circuit Court of Appeals. The ruling was not based on the constitutionality of invoking the name of Jesus, but on whether or not the plaintiffs had legal standing.

26. "Judge Rules Against 'Intelligent Design,'" MSNBC, December 20, 2005, http://www.msnbc.msn.com/id/10545387/ (accessed January 20, 2008).

27. *Dictionary.com*, s.v. "science," http://dictionary.reference.com/browse/science (accessed January 31, 2008).

28. Ibid.

29. Cliff Kincaid, "AIM Report: Former Atheist Says God Exists," Center for Science and Culture, December 21, 2004, http://www.discovery.org/scripts/viewDB/index.php?command=view&program=CSC%20-%20Views%20and%20News&id=2361 (accessed January 20, 2008).

30. Ibid.

31. Ibid.

32. Antony Flew and Gary R. Habermas, "My Pilgrimage from

Atheism to Theism: An Exclusive Interview with Former British Atheist Professor Antony Flew," Biola University, December 9, 2004, http://www.biola.edu/antonyflew/flew-interview.pdf (accessed Januar 20, 2008).

33. Ibid.

34. *Wallace v. Jaffree*, 472 U.S. 38 (1985).

35. Theodore Roosevelt, "Introduction," *Majority Rule and the Judiciary*, ed. William L. Ransom (New York: Charles Scribner's Sons, 1912), 6.

36. Brian Joyce, "Rapist's Prison Sentence Triggers Outrage" WCAX-TV, January 4, 2005, http://www.wcax.com/Global/story.asp?S=4319605 (accessed January 16, 2008).

37. Eric Brown, "National Talk Show Host Blasts Franklin County Judge" WCLT, March 16, 2006, http://www.wclt.com/news/wclt/wclt15840.html (accessed January 16, 2008).

38. "House 1877: Relating to Jessica Lunsford Act," The Florida Senate, September 1, 2005, http://www.flsenate.gov/session/index.cfm?BI_Mode=ViewBillInfo&Mode=Bills&SubMenu=1&Year=2005&billnum=1877 (accessed January 30, 2008). Also see The Jessica Marie Lunsford Foundation at http://www.jmlfoundation.org/.

39. Bill O'Reilly, "Bill's Thoughts on Jessica's Law," *BillOReilly.com*, http://www.billoreilly.com/outragefunnels (accessed January 16, 2008).

40. *Holy Trinity Church v. U.S.*, 143 U.S. 457 (1892).

41. "Abingdon School District v. Schempp," *Common Sense Americanism*, http://www.csamerican.com/SC.asp?r=374+U.S.+203 (accessed March 4, 2008).

42. Gaines, *Perspective*, 98.

43. Federer, *Treasury of Presidential Quotations*, 365.

44. Ellwood P. Clubberley, *Readings in the History of Education: A Collection of Sources and Readings to Illustrate the Development of Educational Practice, Theory, and Organization* (Boston, New York, Chicago: Houghton Mifflin Company, 1920), 292.

45. J. W. Schulte Nordholt, *Woodrow Wilson: A Life for World Peace*, trans. Herbert H. Rowen (Berkeley: University of California Press, 1991), 87.

46. "Constitution Restoration Act of 2005," March 3, 2005, http://www.yuricareport.com/Law%20%26%20Legal/ConstitutionRestorationActOf2005_S520.html#anchor37931 (accessed January 21, 2008).

47. Ibid.

48. Kelly, *Worth Repeating*, 65.

49. Ronald Reagan quote accessed at http://www.presidential-qte.com/ronald-reagan-quotes.html (January 18, 2008).

50. Richard C. S. Trahair, *From Aristotelian to Reaganomics: A Dictionary of Eponyms with Biographies in the Social Sciences* (Westport, CT: Greenwood Press, 1994), 4.

Chapter 7: Anti-Christian Militant Groups

1. "ACLU Defense of Freedom of Religious Practice and Expression," American Civil Liberties Union, November 2007, http://www.aclu.org/religion/govtfunding/26526res20060824.html (accessed February 1, 2008).

2. "Federal Judge Rules Against School-Mandated Prayer at Kentucky High School Graduation Ceremony," American Civil Liberties Union, May 19, 2006, http://www.aclu.org/religion/schools/25616prs20060519.html (accessed February 1, 2008).

3. "Supreme Court Lets Ban on Coerced Prayer at Virginia Military Institute Stand," American Civil Liberties Union, April 26, 2004, http://www.aclu.org/scotus/2003/13910prs20040426.html (accessed February 1, 2008).

4. "West VA School District Ends Graduation Prayer Policy; Students' Lawsuit 'Educated' Officials," American Civil Liberties Union, August 14, 2002, http://www.aclu.org/religion/schools/16161prs20020814.html (accessed February 1, 2008).

5. "In Long-Awaited Victory, High Court Vacates Alabama Decision Allowing Public School Prayer," American Civil Liberties Union, June 26, 2000, http://www.aclu.org/religion/schools/16286prs20000626.html (accessed February 1, 2008).

6. "ACLU Asks Virginia School Boards Not to Open Meetings With Prayer," American Civil Liberties Union, October 1, 1999, http://www.aclu.org/studentsrights/religion/12795prs19991001.html (accessed February 1, 2008).

7. "In Victory for Religious Liberty, Unanimous Appeals Court Finds LA's School Prayer Law Unconstitutional," American Civil Liberties Union, December 12, 2001, http://www.aclu.org/religion/schools/16155prs20011212.html (accessed February 1, 2008).

8. "The Fish Must Go: Court Rules Missouri Must Remove Religious Symbol from City Logo," American Civil Liberties Union, July 9, 1999, http://www.aclu.org/religion/gen/16114prs19990709.html

(accessed February 1, 2008).

9. "Christmas and the ACLU," American Civil Liberties Union, http://www.aclu.org/religion/gen/33210res20071213.html (accessed February 1, 2008).

10. "ACLU Online Video Examines Roe v. Wade's Importance for Civil Liberties, 35 Years Later," American Civil Liberties Union, January 22, 2008, http://aclu.org/reproductiverights/abortion/33746prs20080122.html (accessed February 1, 2008).

11. "In the Courts: The Year Ahead for Reproductive Rights," American Civil Liberties Union, January 22, 2008, http://www.aclu.org/reproductiverights/abortion/33720res20080122.html (accessed February 1, 2008).

12. "ACLU Calls Flag Desecration Amendment Assault on Free Speech; Says Measure Fails Very Principles Flag Embodies," American Civil Liberties Union, May 25, 2005, http://www.aclu.org/freespeech/flag/11269prs20050525.html (accessed February 1, 2008).

13. "In the Courts: The Year Ahead for Reproductive Rights."

14. "In Stunning Civil Rights Victory, VT Court Directs State to Give Same-Sex Couples Marriage Benefits," American Civil Liberties Union, December 20, 1999, http://www.aclu.org/lgbt/relationships/11979prs19991220.html (accessed February 1, 2008).

15. "Maryland Court Says State Cannot Bar Same-Sex Couples from Marriage Protections," American Civil Liberties Union, January 20, 2006, http://www.aclu.org/lgbt/relationships/23558prs20060120.html (accessed February 1, 2008).

16. "ACLU Messages Points on Marriage for Same-Sex Couples and the Federal Marriage Amendment," American Civil Liberties Union, November 2003, http://www.aclu.org/getequal/ffm/section1/1a2points.pdf (accessed February 1, 2008).

17. Stephanie Strom, "The A.C.L.U. Rejects Foundation Grants Over Terror Language," *The New York Times*, October 19, 2004.

18. Hans Zieger, "Pledge Allegiance to the ACLU," August 16, 2003, http://www.newswithviews.com/DesAme/ destroy.htm (accessed January 18, 2008).

19. Ben Stein, "Stuff Ben Wrote: Christmas," December 18, 2005, http://www.benstein.com/121805xmas.html (accessed January 18, 2008).

20. "ACLU Messages Points on Marriage for Same-Sex Couples and the Federal Marriage Amendment," American Civil Liberties Union.

21. "School Prayer Decision," *American Atheists*, 2006, http://www.atheists.org/Courthouse/prayer.html (accessed January 21, 2008).

22. Council for Secular Humanism.

23. Limbaugh, *Persecution*, 65.

24. "Major Religions of the World Ranked by Number of Adherents," Adherents.com, http://www.adherents.com/Religions_By_Adherents.html (accessed February 1, 2008). According to the site, Christianity has 2.1 billion adherents, while the Secular/Nonreligious/Agnostic/Atheistic category is ranked third with 1.1 billion.

25. "The List: The World's Fastest-Growing Religions," *Foreign Policy Magazine*, May 2007, http://www.foreignpolicy.com/story/cms.php?story_id=3835 (accessed February 1, 2008).

26. Brigitte Gabriel, *Because They Hate: A Survivor of Islamic Terror Warns America* (New York: St. Martin's Press, 2006), x.

27. Oliver North, "Media Madness," *The Conservative Voice*, March 2, 2006, http://www.theconservativevoice.com/article/12780.html (accessed January 18, 2008).

28. "Burger King Recalls 'Sacrilegious' Desserts," *The Scotsman*, September 17, 2005, http://news.scotsman.com/latestnews/Burger-King-recalls-sacrilegious-desserts.2662082.jp (accessed February 1, 2008).

29. James Joyner, "Things that Offend Muslims: Cartoons, Books, History, Operas . . . ," *Outside the Beltway*, September 27, 2006, http://www.outsidethebeltway.com/archives/2006/09/things_that_offend_muslims_cartoons_books_history_operas_/ (accessed February 1, 2008).

30. Alexandra Frean, "Three Pigs Story Ruled 'Offense to Muslims,'" *The Times*, January 24, 2008, http://entertainment.timesonline.co.uk/tol/arts_and_entertainment/books/children/article3241394.ece (accessed February 1, 2008).

31. Barbara G. Baker, "Young Muslims in Turkey Murder Three Christians," *Christianity Today*, April 20, 2007, http://www.christianitytoday.com/ct/2007/aprilweb-only/116-52.0.html (accessed February 1, 2008).

32. "130 Christians Murdered Over Cartoons: Muslim Rioters Rampage through Nigerian Villages," *WorldNetDaily*, February 24, 2006, http://www.worldnetdaily.com/news/article.asp?ARTICLE_ID=48973 (accessed February 1, 2008).

33. "Six Christians Murdered by Muslim Mob in Ethiopia," *Christian News Wire*, November 30, 2006, http://christiannewswire

.com/news/24371627.html (accessed February 26, 2008).

34. D. Cooney, "Afghan Christian Could Get Death Sentence: Afghan Man Prosecuted for Converting From Islam to Christianity," *AP News Service*, March 19, 2006.

35. Judith Apter Klinghoffer, "Selective Muslim Silence," History News Network, October 31, 2005, http://hnn.us/articles/17589.html (accessed February 1, 2008).

Chapter 8: Federal Government Encroachment

1. Kelly, *Worth Repeating*, 128.

2. Jay Sekulow, "The IRS Should Collect Taxes, Not Be the 'Speech Police,'" American Center for Law & Justice, http://www.aclj.org/media/pdf/040900_JAY_churches_political_speech.pdf (accessed January 21, 2008).

3. Ibid.

4. Ibid.

5. Robert Bork, "Our Judicial Oligarchy," *First Things: A Monthly Journal of Religion and Public Life* (November 1996): 67.

6. Ivo H. Daalder and I. M. Destler, et al, "Assessing the Department of Homeland Security," The Brookings Institute, July 2002, http://www.publicpolicy.umd.edu/faculty/destler/assessdhs.pdf (accessed February 2, 2008).

7. "Search and Seizure," The Rutherford Institute, http://www.rutherford.org/Issues/SearchAndSeizure.asp (accessed February 2, 2008).

8. Nisha N. Mohammed, "In Recent Letter to Congress and New Book from Greenhaven Press, Rutherford Institute President Calls for Broad Review of Patriot Act," The Rutherford Institute, April 27, 2005, http://rutherford.org/articles_db/press_release.asp?article_id=549 (accessed February 2, 2008).

9. "The End of America: May 10, 2005," *JPFO Alerts*, May 11, 2005, http://www.jpfo.org/alerts/alert20050511.htm (accessed January 18, 2008).

10. Bruce Schneier, "Real ID," *Crypto-Gram Newsletter*, May 15, 2005, http://www.schneier.com/crypto-gram-0505.html#2 (accessed January 18, 2008).

11. Ibid.

12. Bruce Schneier, "More on Real ID," *Crypto-Gram Newsletter*, May 15, 2007, http://www.schneier.com/crypto-gram-0705.html#6 (accessed January 18, 2008).

13. "Homeland Security Department Announces Deeply Flawed Regulations for National ID System," Electronic Privacy Information Center, January 11, 2008, http://epic.org/press/011108.html (accessed January 18, 2008).

14. Paul Weyrich, "DHS and Voter Identification Problem," Townhall.com, January 16, 2008, http://www.townhall.com/columnists/PaulWeyrich/2008/01/16/dhs_and_the_voter_identification_problem (accessed February 2, 2008).

15. Ronald Reagan quote accessed at http://www.presidential-qte.com/ronald-reagan-quotes.html (January 17, 2008).

16. Ronald Reagan, "A Time for Choosing," *Classics of American Political and Constitutional Thought, Volume 2: Reconstruction to the Present*, ed. Scott J. Hammond, Kevin R. Hardwick, Howard L. Lubert (Indianapolis: Hackett Publishing, 2007), 674.

17. Cook, *The Book of Positive Quotations*, 507.

Chapter 9: Anti-Israel Political Forces

1. Tracey Rich, "The Land of Israel," *Judaism 101*, http://www.jewfaq.org/israel.htm (accessed February 3, 2008).

2. Mark Twain, "Concerning the Jews," *How to Tell a Story and Other Essays* (Hartford, CT: The American Publishing Company, 1908), 275.

3. Robert Stearns, "Why Israel Matters," *Charisma*, May 2006, http://www.charismamag.com/display.php?id=12885 (accessed January 18, 2008).

4. Mark Tessler and Jamal Sanad, "Will the Arab Public Accept Peace with Israel? Evidence from Surveys in Three Arab Societies," *Israel at the Crossroad*, ed. Efraim Karsh and Gregory Mahler (London, New York: British Academic Press, 1994), 50.

5. Andrew Duncan, "Land for Peace: Israel's Choice," *Between Warn and Peace: Dilemmas of Israeli Security*, ed. Efraim Karsh (London: Frank Cass, 1996), 59.

6. Ofira Seliktar, *Divided We Stand: American Jews, Israel, and the Peace Process* (Westport, CT: Praeger, 2002), 123.

7. "Israel's Best Minds Have Lost Faith in the Possibility of Peace," *The National Post*, July 2002, reprinted at FactsOfIsrael.com, July 20, 2002, http://www.factsofisrael.com/blog/archives/000207.html (accessed February 3, 2008).

8. Tessler and Sanad, "Will the Public Accept...," 49.

9. Ibid., 50.

10. Seliktar, *Divided We Stand*, 207.

11. John Hagee and David Brog, "Israel and the Role of Christians," *Ventures in Success*, http://www.hisbranch.com/Israel.html (accessed January 19, 2008). This quote may also be found in John Hagee, *Jerusalem Countdown* (Lake Mary, FL: Frontline, 2006).

12. John McTernan and Bill Koenig, *Israel: The Blessing or the Curse* (Oklahoma City: Hearthstone Publishing, 2002).

13. Hagee, *Jerusalem Countdown*, 86.

14. Margaret Coker and Irris Makler, "Israel Evicts Settlers in Day of Tears, Violence," *Cox News Service*, September 19, 2005, http://www.coxwashington.com/reporters/content/reporters/stories/2005/09/18/ISRAEL_GAZA18_COX.html (accessed January 19, 2008).

Chapter 10: Christian Apathy

1. Kevin Wayne Johnson, *Give God the Glory! Called to Be Light in the Workplace* (Hillsborough, NJ: Writing for the Lord Ministries, 2003), 130.

2. Stearns, "Why Israel Matters."

3. Bill Kristol, "Dyspepsia on the Right," *New York Times*, February 4, 2008, http://www.nytimes.com/2008/02/04/opinion/04kristol.html?_r=2&ex=1359867600&en=6261f07b1542c95d&ei=5088&partner=rssnyt&emc=rss&oref=slogin&oref=slogin (accessed February 4, 2008).

4. Ravenhill, *America Is Too Young to Die*, 102.

5. J. Lee Grady, "Clouds without Water," *Charisma*, May 2006, http://www.charismamag.com/display.php?id=12866 (accessed January 20, 2008).

6. Ibid.

7. Andy Stern, *A Country that Works: Getting Back on Track* (New York: Free Press, 2006), 117.

8. Mary Johnson and Carol Rittner, "Anne Frank in the World: A Study Guide," *Anne Frank in the World: Essays and Reflections*, ed. Carol Rittner (Armonk, New York: M. E. Sharpe, 1998), 115.

9. Elizabeth Barrett Browning, *Aurora Leigh,* Book vii, in John Bartlett, *Familiar Quotations,* 10th Ed., http://www.bartleby.com/100/446.html#446.note3 (accessed January 19, 2008).

10. Limbaugh, *Persecution*, 6–7.

11. Abraham Lincoln, "Reply to Loyal Colored People of Baltimore upon Presentation of a Bible, September 7, 1864," *The Collected Works*

of Abraham Lincoln, Vol. 7, ed. Roy P. Basler (New Brunswick, NJ: Rutgers University Press, 1953), 543.

12. "Calling Christmas By Its Name: People Are Saying 'Happy Holidays' Instead of 'Merry Christmas,'" *ABC News*, December 11, 2005, http://abcnews.go.com/GMA/ChristmasCountdown/story?id=1394841 (accessed February 1, 2008).

13. Peter Lattman, "Federal Judge Samuel Kent Reprimanded By Fifth Circuit," *The Wall Street Journal*, October 1, 2007, http://blogs.wsj.com/law/2007/10/01/federal-judge-samuel-kent-reprimanded-by-fifth-circuit/ (accessed January 20, 2008).

14. According to Rick Casey, "Feds to Seal Evidence Against Judge," *Houston Chronicle*, October 3, 2007, http://www.chron.com/disp/story.mpl/metropolitan/casey/5175407.html (accessed January 20, 2008).

Chapter 11: Divine Judgment

1. U. S. Grant, *Personal Memoirs of U. S. Grant,* Vol. 1 (New York: Charles R. Webster & Company, 1885), 56.

2. Henry, ed., *Patrick Henry: Life, Correspondence and Speeches,* Vol. III, 449.

3. "Glimpses of American History," Christian History Institute, March 2007, http://chi.gospelcom.net/GLIMPSEF/Glimpses/glmps041.shtml (accessed February 5, 2008).

4. Ben Stein, "Something's Happening Here," November 14, 2007, http://somethings-happening-here.blogspot.com/ 2007/11/ben-stein.html (accessed January 20, 2008).

5. Franklin, "For Prayers in the Convention," 600–601.

Chapter 12: Return to God's Destiny

1. Ravenhill, *America Is Too Young to Die*, 105.

2. Jonathan Edwards, *A History of the Work of Redemption, in The Works of President Edwards In Ten Volumes*, Vol. III (New York: G. & C. & H. Carvill, 1830), 221.

3. Charles G. Finney, *Lectures on Revivals of Religion,* 2nd Ed. (New York: Leavitt, Lord & Co., 1835), 249.

4. Gerald McDermott, "The 18th-Century Awakening: A Reminder for American Evangelicals in the 1990s," http://www.honeywagonseptic.com/Study%20Items/Studies/revival/wakeup.html (accessed January 20, 2008).

5. H. L. Wilmington, *Wilmington's Guide to the Bible* (Wheaton, IL: Tyndale House, 1981), 561.

6. McDermott, "The 18th Century Awakening."

7. Ibid.

8. Curtis Hutson, *Punch Lines: A Collection of One-Liners, Sentence-Sermons, and Attention-Getters* (Murfreesboro, TN: Sword of the Lord Publishers, 1989), 33.

9. Lewis V. Baldwin, *There Is a Balm in Gilead: The Cultural Roots of Martin Luther King, Jr.* (Minneapolis: Fortress Press, 1991), 325.

10. David O. Dykes, *Character out of Chaos: Daring to Be a Daniel in Today's World* (Grand Rapids, MI: Kregel, 2004), 111.

11. Bruce Schreiner, "Graduates Defy Judge's Prayer Ban at Ky. High School," *Associated Press*, May 21, 2006, http://www.christianpost.com/article/20060521/22036_Graduates_Defy_Judge%27s_Prayer_Ban_at_Ky._High_School.htm (accessed January 20, 2008).

12. Ravenhill, *America Is Too Young to Die*, 99–100.

Chapter 13: Awake, America!

1. Daniel Webster, *The Works of Daniel Webster,* Vol. IV (Boston: Little, Brown, and Company, 1890), 47.

2. Rev. Carl Richardson, "The Boat's On Fire." Used by permission.

To Contact the Author

Robert White
P.O. Box 130938
Tyler, TX 75713
903-566-6484
www.awakeamerica.us